Norm LeMay & Steven Kaufman

To Mick
Toss That Trash!
Steven Kauf

THE GARBAGEMAN'S GUIDE TO LIFE

HOW TO GET OUT OF THE DUMPS

Eight Steps to Clear Your Mind
and Jumpstart Your Life

NEW YORK

THE GARBAGEMAN'S GUIDE TO LIFE
HOW TO GET OUT OF THE DUMPS

Published in New York, New York, by Morgan James Publishing. Morgan James and The Entrepreneurial Publisher are trademarks of Morgan James, LLC. www.MorganJamesPublishing.com

The Morgan James Speakers Group can bring authors to your live event. For more information or to book an event visit The Morgan James Speakers Group at www.TheMorganJamesSpeakersGroup.com.

The Garbageman's Guide, LLC
7327 SW Barnes Road
Suite 713
Portland, OR 97225
(800) 806-0301

www.TheGarbagemansGuide.com

ISBN 9781614487937   paperback
ISBN 9781614487944   eBook
Library of Congress Control Number: 2013944429

The authors fervently believe in the concept of reuse and recycling and in the preservation of our natural resources. While they talk about throwing away trash in this book, it is only as a metaphor for getting rid of mental garbage and is not intended to endorse environmentally unfriendly habits. Readers are encouraged to participate in local recycling efforts and to minimize their own waste production as much as possible.

BitLit
FOR ALL THE COPIES YOU OWN

FREE eBook edition for your existing eReader with purchase

PRINT NAME ABOVE

For more information, instructions, restrictions, and to register your copy, go to www.bitlit.ca/readers/register or use your QR Reader to scan the barcode.

In an effort to support local communities, and to raise awareness and funds, Morgan James Publishing donates a percentage of all book sales for the life of each book to Habitat for Humanity Peninsula and Greater Williamsburg.

Get involved today. Visit
www.MorganJamesBuilds.com.

Habitat for Humanity
Peninsula and Greater Williamsburg
Building Partner

DEDICATION

I dedicate this book to my wife, Vicki, who thinks in tandem
with me and without whom there would be no Garbageman's
Guide to Life. I also dedicate this to the industry that my father
introduced me to and that touches everyone's life.
—NAL

FOR ABIGAIL
You're my sun and my stars;
My moon and my sea;
And I love you.
—SDK

TABLE OF CONTENTS

INTRODUCTION

"Success is learning how to be comfortable
with being uncomfortable."
—Anonymous

You wouldn't believe what I learn from the garbage people throw away.

I know when someone is seriously ill by the sudden increase in medical packaging in their trash. I know when a couple is getting divorced because of all the memorabilia they're throwing out. I know which Christmas toys are junk when I see the same broken pieces one house after another. So much of what people buy eventually flows through my truck. And it tells a story—the history of a life, one piece of garbage at a time.

I've learned a lot from these stories over the years—lessons that can help everyone. Now, it wouldn't surprise me if you're thinking, "Come on. He's just a guy who empties trash for a living. What can I possibly learn from him?" Here's the truth: You spend your time and energy deciding what you're going to bring *into* your life. I see what happens after you *get rid of it*. That gives me a point of view that most people don't think about: what the world is like when the things in our lives reach the end of the line.

Listen, I know I'm invisible most of the time. People hardly give me a second thought, even though I'm driving a huge, fifty-ton truck through their neighborhood. I also realize that if someone were to ask you where you find inspiration, "from my garbage-man" probably wouldn't be your first answer. Yet, I provide a service that's absolutely essential. Imagine what life would be like if garbage collection just stopped. What I do is as important to society as producing food and generating electricity. At the same time, this job has been highly personal to me. I've had the opportunity to visit thousands of houses week in and week out. I've watched families grow and change, and learned incredible lessons about the flow of trash and the flow of life—all without you even knowing my name.

I never thought I'd be part of something this important. I just wanted to be a garbageman. But after so long on the job, I began to notice some pretty powerful symbolism in almost every part of waste hauling. Here's a perfect example.

A while back, construction crews tore down an ugly old apartment building near the center of my town. All that was left was a big open lot. I couldn't believe how different everything looked once that eyesore was gone. I found myself wondering what was going to fill that empty space. A new restaurant? Some cool little stores? A newer, more modern apartment building? The possibilities seemed endless. Then I realized something interesting. The value of that property went up because of what was taken away, not what was added. That got me thinking.

What if I did the same thing with the thoughts, beliefs, and opinions I have in my head—that nagging voice in the background that causes all the doubt and the second-guessing? What would life look like if I got rid of those just like the construction company got rid of that building?

I'll tell you, it would be pretty amazing. Where once I had piles of garbage telling me what I couldn't do, I'd now have a ton of empty space, mental breathing room that could change my inner landscape just like the empty lot changed the look of the neighborhood. I'd see a million new possibilities that the trash used to hide. Is it time to go back to school? Raise money for that volunteer project I've been dreaming about? Start training for that half-marathon I always wanted to do? Without all the mental chatter, what I truly want is closer than ever. It sounds a little backward, but I'd *get* more by *giving up* more.

> IT SOUNDS A LITTLE BACKWARD, BUT I'D GET MORE BY GIVING UP MORE.

As I kicked this around, I got pretty excited. Taking out my mental garbage could make room for how I really want to live my life. No more trash that stops me. No more chaos screaming in my ear and pulling me off track. No more beating my head against the wall, doing the same silly things over and over again. Instead, I'd have a chance to *finally* sit in my own driver's seat and steer my truck in the direction I want. That seems like a pretty good deal!

It doesn't mean an end to garbage in my life. I've been creating it from the time I was little and I'll be creating it until the day I die. This isn't about making trash go away. *It's about choosing whether my garbage will continue to control my life.* It's a chance to say, "Enough, already! I'm not going to think and act this way anymore!"

I went through a few nasty breakups when I first started dating, so I got it into my head that I was lousy at relationships and just gave up. After all my buddies started finding these great women to date, I finally said to myself, "Come on. This idea that you're lousy at relationships is baloney." I cleared that old trash away and started going out again. And wouldn't you know it? A few months later, I met my beautiful wife.

If I had let my head keep filling with *I suck at dating* thoughts, I might have missed out on marriage and never been a part of this great family that we've built. If I think negative, that's all I'm going to see and experience. However, if I get rid of that trash and fill my head with positive thoughts, beliefs, and opinions, I'll be a lot happier. What I've gradually come to realize is that I have *total and complete control* over this choice between garbage and freedom. Once I started to play with this idea, a process began to emerge: eight simple steps to get rid of mental trash, all of which mirror the way I deal with trash on my route.

1. **Find the Value and Toss That Trash**
   Learn about the critical role your Value Filter™ plays in helping to decide what to keep and what to toss.

2. **Keep It Empty**
   Do amazing things with the empty space that's left over once inner trash is thrown out.

3. **Create Your Route**
   Determine the direction your life can go.

4. **Park Your Ego**
   Learn how to keep ego on the side of the road so goals can be reached.

5. **Leave It in the Landfill**
   Overcome the urge to dig up old trash once it's finally thrown away.

6. **Get Away From Toxic Waste**
   Avoid the pitfalls of being trapped by hazardous relationships and toxic situations.

7. **Stop Hoarding**
   Jump into action when collecting inner trash gets out of hand.

8. **Take Care of Your Truck**

Keep your body on the road and in great operating condition.

When I look at these eight steps, all the pieces of waste management—the truck, the garbage can, and the landfill—are part of a larger metaphor to help me dump my mental trash. As strange as it may sound, the simple act of throwing away my trash permanently changed the way I think and act.

Here's the great part: I didn't have to learn anything new to put this into action! The same skills I use to empty trash in the physical world are the exact same ones I use to get rid of trash everywhere else in my life. From the time I was a kid, I learned how to look at something, weigh its value, and decide if it was garbage or not. If it was trash, I knew how to get rid of it: Toss it into the nearest can, empty all the cans into the big one in the garage, and drag the big one to the curb every Sunday night. Once I became a garbageman, I realized that getting rid of all my trash, whether it's in my house or my head, is just as easy. That's the knowledge I want to pass on to you.

Take a moment and think about emptying non-physical garbage: things like a bad experience or a relationship that went badly. That's how we'll be talking about emptying garbage from this point forward.

I remember the last time I cleaned out the hallway closet. I hardly thought about what I was doing: keep, toss, toss, keep. Piles appeared and garbage bags were filled up. In an hour, the project was done. Well, if you look a little closer, here's what I was actually doing.

First, my brain got very clear about a definition of value. It hammered out the criteria for *what to keep* and *what to toss*. Then, it evaluated every item in that closet and made a simple decision: If it had no value, it was garbage. Before I knew it, the trash was gone and the closet was nearly empty. And nothing new made it back in there unless it met the criteria of "valuable." It's been nearly a year and the closet is still in great shape.

Cleaning out the contents of my head works exactly the same way. I start by deciding what makes one thought valuable and another opinion useless. Then, I examine the thoughts in my head, decide which ones aren't valuable anymore, and toss them—beliefs like *I could never run a marathon* or *I'd make a lousy volunteer.* If a new thought wants to jump into that emptiness I just created, it had better be hooked to what I really want out of my life or it's gone as soon as it shows up. That's how the first three steps work. They form a fast, super-efficient cycle that continually dumps any thought, belief, or opinion that has no value to me anymore.

The remaining five steps in the framework are like caution signs that can interrupt the cycle of the first three steps. Ego, persistent garbage, toxic waste, hoarding, and not taking care of myself—each of these can slow me down and prevent me from dumping my mental garbage.

So forget about the myth that improving yourself is a long, complicated, drawn-out process. Like I said earlier, if you can drag your can to the curb, you can get rid of the rest of the trash in your life. And if you think the desire to improve yourself means there's something wrong with you, try this on: You're reading this book because of what's *right* with you. I want to make more money. I want more happiness at home. I want to achieve more on the job. If I'm doing something that's holding me back from getting those things—like letting my trash run my life—I want to know about it so I can fix it. I have a lot I want to accomplish. I sure don't want a big pile of garbage to be the only thing that kept me from my dreams.

I want to be clear about something. I realize that tough times create tough emotional garbage. I've faced the same things you have: heartaches, disappointments, and tragedies that have shaped the person I am today. I can't just roll that stuff to the curb and say, "It's out of my life." It's going to take some work. All I ask is that you hang in there with me. Try a few of the techniques. Think about some of the lessons. Wrestle with some of the exercises. It's all part of you discovering your own Inner Garbageman™.

When I talk about getting rid of emotional garbage, you're going to hear me use phrases like "throw it out" or "put it in your personal landfill." Sometimes, it may make more sense to recycle a thought into something more useful or reuse a belief or opinion in a different way. To me, recycling, reusing, and throwing out all mean the same thing: *getting emotional garbage out of my life.*

There's another important point to remember. I'm not saying that all of the beliefs and opinions in my head are bad. Some might be sentimental or make me feel great about myself. Those are the thoughts that have value. The trick is figuring out which ones keep me on track and which ones torpedo what I want out of life. This is critical because I've learned that what I think and what I do is what I will become. If I think that diet and exercise don't matter, I'll eat donuts and sit on the couch, gaining weight. If I believe that good health is a priority, I'll eat more vegetables, hit the gym three times a week, and watch my weight. So deciding which opinions to keep and which beliefs to toss can have a big effect on the way my life unfolds—good or bad.

> I'M NOT SAYING THAT ALL OF THE BELIEFS AND OPINIONS IN MY HEAD ARE BAD.

There's a great Cherokee story that really hammers this point home. An old chief was teaching his grandson about life. "A fight is going on inside me," he said to the boy. "It is a terrible fight between two wolves. One is evil—he is anger, envy, sorrow, regret, greed, arrogance, self-pity, guilt, resentment, inferiority, lies, false pride, superiority, self-doubt, and ego. The other is good—he is joy, peace, love, hope, serenity, humility, kindness, benevolence, empathy, generosity, truth, compassion, and faith. This same fight is going on inside you—and inside every other person."

The grandson thought about it for a minute and then asked his grandfather, "Which wolf will win?"

The old chief simply replied, "The one you feed."

Holding on to my old garbage is a choice. So is the decision to get rid of it. I know I can't flip a switch and *poof*—all those powerful memories and feelings are gone. Is it going to take commitment and hard work to toss them? Absolutely. Am I going to run into setbacks, disappointments, and frustration along the way? I guarantee I will.

At the same time, this is my life! All the choices I've made have led me to this point, and all the choices I'm about to make will lead me somewhere else. Where do I want that place to be? And since there's nothing that's forcing me to keep certain thoughts, beliefs, and opinions in my head, it all boils down to a simple, fundamental question: *Am I willing to end garbage collection in my mind?* If the answer is yes, my life is going to be different. I invite you to make the same choice and tap into your Inner Garbageman. Imagine what you could accomplish without all that trash!

I remember being taught in science class that waste removal is one of the elements essential for life. It's a basic necessity, something we all have to do every day in order to thrive. That leads to one of the two central themes in this book: *We are all garbagemen.* You carry your family's trash to the curb; I carry the community's trash to the landfill. You decide what to keep and toss, and so do I. By harnessing your garbageman's skills and throwing away all the unwanted trash in your life, you can change your world forever.

The other central theme is that *we all need empty space.* Have you ever ridden a subway during rush hour? Fought your way through a crowded bar? Navigated the throngs of people at a major sporting event? Remember how it felt when you walked through the front door and out into the open? That's the rush of emptiness, and your mind needs exactly the same thing. If you keep your head crammed full of the same thoughts year after year, it's hard to chart a clear course for yourself. On the other hand, if you regularly toss the useless thoughts you don't need anymore, you open up room for your future—one that you have the power and control to shape.

There's an old Zen fable about the time Nan-in, a Japanese master, received a visit from a university professor who wanted to know more about Zen. Nan-in poured him a cup of tea—and kept pouring and pouring until the tea was overflowing and spilling onto the table.

"It's full!" the professor shouted. "There's no room for any more tea!"

"That's correct," Nan-in said. "You are like this cup, full of your own opinions. How can I show you Zen unless you first empty yourself?"

In all my years of watching what flows through the back of my truck, I've learned that it's better to empty out than to fill up. That's what I want for you: the opportunity for every area of your life to be clean and trash-free, so you have room to create the future you've always wanted. So let's get started and learn how to unleash your Inner Garbageman!

HOW TO USE THIS BOOK

"No farmer ever plowed a field by turning it over in his mind."
—*George E. Woodbury*

There's a lot of great information in this guide, and I want to make sure you get every single ounce of value out of it. So before I get started with Step 1, I want to show you a number of different ways you can use this book.

READ IT

People read books in different ways. Some folks start on page 1 and read methodically until the last word. Some like to skip around, while others like to skim first, then jump in later. I've designed this book around all of these different reading styles.

> EACH CHAPTER COVERS ONE OF THE EIGHT STEPS OF TOSSING MENTAL TRASH.

Each chapter covers one of the eight steps of tossing mental trash. Like other guides, chapters build on each another. However, each chapter is like a mini-book that can stand on its own. If you want to read them out of order, or come back at a later time and brush up on a single topic, go for it. You'll get a ton of value that way.

If you do read out of order and you run across an unfamiliar term, just flip to the glossary at the end of the book. You'll find definitions for the most common words we use in each of the eight steps.

If you don't feel like reading a chapter from start to finish, I've still got you covered. Chapters are broken into small sections. Feel free to scan the headings until you find a topic that interests you. Also, on many of the pages, you'll see quotes from certain parts of the chapter. You can skim those to get a brief snapshot of what each step is about.

Now, I don't know about you, but I don't like reading a book that tells me what I should and shouldn't be doing. I learn more when the authors talk about their own successes and failures. That gives me the freedom I need to pick through what's being said, try on the parts that I think are most important, and keep the ones that fit me the best. That's exactly how this book is written. It's mostly me sharing what I've learned after a lot of years picking up everyone's trash. Use what you think is helpful and throw out the rest. At the end of the day, you're the best person to decide what's right for your personality and for the trash that you're carrying around.

> USE WHAT YOU THINK IS HELPFUL AND THROW OUT THE REST.

You'll also see some boxes with a garbage can icon. Inside each box, I'll be asking you specific questions that I hope will get you thinking about what's in the chapter. I follow that up with an action plan: specific ideas designed to help you put each step in to motion.

Finally, every chapter has a section called "Use Caution." These are specific trouble spots that could knock the action plan off course. Have a look at them, and then keep them in the back of your mind. They may come in handy someday.

WRITE IN IT

I wanted to give you a practical, no-nonsense way to take the content of each chapter and apply it directly to your own life. It's one thing to hear me talk. It's way better if you can take what you've learned and really make it your own. That's why each chapter has a section called "Taking It to the Street." As I like to say, this is where the rubber meets the road.

"Taking It to the Street" is a series of questions and exercises that takes the action plan and puts it to work right away. To get the most out of this section, I highly recommend that you grab a pen and answer the questions by writing in the book. That's right. Scribble away! This is one time you really want to write in the textbook!

Have you heard the expression "What occupies your mind ends up expanding into your life"? "Taking It to the Street" offers you a chance to put down the manual, pick up the wrench, and do the work yourself. That's where it's going to do the most good—and where you'll get the best results.

USE IT

There's no quiz or test at the end of this book. *The Garbageman's Guide to Life* is not about memorizing a formula. It's about changing your life. Use what you need from this material—in whatever amount is best for you. I recommend that you simply try out this idea of dumping your mental trash and see what happens. I've gotten some great results from these eight steps, and I'd love it if the same happened for you.

Also, remember that you're working with real garbage every day. Put that to work for you. Whenever you pass by a trash can or you see a garbage truck rumble down your street, let it remind you of a concept from this book. That's a great way to keep the material alive.

STAY WITH IT

Whenever I start something new—a diet or an exercise routine—my enthusiasm is usually off the chart. I jump in with both feet and, for a week or two, I live and breathe the new program. Then, life creeps back in and the enthusiasm fades—especially if I didn't get immediate results.

Dumping mental trash takes staying power—more than a day or a week. The more you commit yourself to emptying your old garbage, the easier it is to stay with it. So don't lose sight of your goal: a clutter-free life. *Keep tossing your trash!*

SHARE IT

Want a great way to get the garbage out of your life? Give copies of the book to everyone on your team: your family, your friends, and your co-workers. Just like exercising with a partner, it's a lot easier to stay motived when someone else is working on the same goal with you.

I also encourage you to visit our website at GG-Resources.com. There are a ton of useful tools that will take this material to a whole new level. If the idea of dumping your mental trash is really inspiring to you, the website is a great place to keep learning and exploring.

The authors of this book—Norm LeMay and Steven Kaufman— would also *love it* if you would share your experience with them. What results have you been getting from the eight steps? How has it changed the way you think and act? Send an email to MyExperience@TheGarbagemansGuide.com and let them know how this book has impacted you.

Finally, I want to know what else we can do to help you get rid of your mental garbage. Is there a topic you'd like to read more about? What kind of audio courses or webinars would you like to see? Tell us what tools you need to empty your mental trash and we will do our utmost to create them for you.

LIVE IT

In our own way, each of us is a garbageman, taking out the trash and doing our best to keep ourselves uncluttered. I've found that doing the same thing for my mind has made an enormous difference, and I want that for you, too. Read it. Write it. Use it. Stay with it. Share it. But most important: *Live it*. That's where you find the route to the life you've always wanted to have.

START HERE:
IT'S TIME TO ACT

"Faith is the daring of the soul to go farther than it can see."
—*William Newton Clark*

Before we jump into a discussion of the eight steps, I want to share something with you—the most important lesson I've learned in my journey of getting rid of mental trash. It's what makes the eight steps of getting rid of mental trash so effective.

Ordinarily, I wouldn't start off a conversation about getting rid of garbage by talking about cats, but a while back, my neighbor was going on vacation, and I was in charge of taking care of Bubba, his old fat feline that he'd had for years. The first day, I let myself in, filled up the bowl with food, and cleaned out the litter box. I called out the cat's name a hundred times—"Bubba! Bubba!"—thinking he'd want a little company. When he didn't answer, I got a little nervous. Was he okay? Had he escaped? I looked all around the house—everywhere I thought a cat would hide—but I never found him.

I show up the second day, and the same thing: no cat. The food was gone, and the litter box had been used, so I knew he was in the house somewhere. That's how it went for the next two weeks: I knew the cat was okay, but I never saw hide nor hair of that little fur ball.

When my neighbor came back, I told him what had happened, and he just laughed. "He was probably on one of the dining room chairs. He loves to hide in plain sight."

Boy, did that get me thinking. How many times have I missed something that's right in front of me—especially with the thoughts, beliefs, and opinions, or "TBOs" that are floating around in my brain? They've been with me for so long, and I'm so used to how they influence the way I act that I don't notice them hiding in plain sight, just like that cat.

> I CAN'T KICK OFF THE EIGHT STEPS OF DUMPING MY MENTAL TRASH WITHOUT FIRST PAYING MORE ATTENTION TO WHAT I AM THINKING.

That's the lesson of the Bubba story. Before I can figure out which of my TBOs are trash, I first have to pay attention to the TBOs themselves. I have to notice what's taking up space inside my head, but hiding from me in plain sight. It seems like an obvious thing to do: You can't fix a problem until you know what the problem is. That's what made me realize that I can't kick off the eight steps of dumping my mental trash without *first* paying more attention to what I am thinking.

So I asked myself, "How in the world do I do that?" Then I realized that I already knew how! I'm a garbageman, right? I'm already tuned into trash. I know when someone's getting ready to move or when a family has had a baby by what they throw out. If I used that same skill and tuned into the trash I'm hauling around in my head, I could do myself a lot of good.

So I came up with a three-step process that I call "ACT": Aware, Choose, and Toss.

"Aware" means noticing what I'm thinking; it means turning up the volume on my TBOs a notch or two so I can actually hear them. It's moving from the subconscious to the conscious, from white noise to front brain. This means the next time I call myself an idiot or I tell myself that I'm not good enough, I actually notice what I'm doing: running my self-worth through the shredder. Here's why that's so powerful.

I remember the day I found out there was no Santa Claus and no Tooth Fairy. From that moment forward, the database of information in my head was changed forever. No matter how much my little-kid brain wanted to *unlearn* what I'd just been taught, there was no going back. That's what "Aware" does: It makes me permanently notice the way I think and act.

That's when "Choose" kicks in. Once I'm aware, then I have the power to choose what I want to do next. Do I continue to let thoughts of *I'm not good enough* stop me from applying for that supervisor's job that's opening up? Or do I choose to say, "I'm done with that thought right now because it's not doing me any good" and move on to the third step of ACT: "Toss" that garbage right out of my mind? When I do that, I can move on to Step 1: the mechanics of picking out trash and getting rid of it. Once I'm aware of what I'm thinking, it becomes so much easier to spot the garbage and choose to let it go. If the same trash pops back into my head farther down the road, no problem. Now that I'm aware of it, I'll be able to spot it faster the second time, then the third time, until the chokehold that trash has on me is broken.

If I were to boil ACT down to one concept, it's about separating myself from my garbage. I don't want this stuff hanging around in my head any more than I want it hanging around in the kitchen or the garage. Being aware of what I'm thinking really helps me see the places where I'm letting the garbage

IT'S ABOUT SEPARATING MYSELF FROM MY GARBAGE.

take over. I have so many great things I want to get done in this life. The farther I get away from my garbage, the better the chances are that I can really accomplish them.

So as you start diving into the eight steps, be aware of what you're thinking. Notice what's floating through your brain. Ask yourself what effect the junk is having on your life, how it's influencing the choices you make, and where it's holding you back. When you put ACT to work for you, you'll see how much it can clear your mind and jumpstart your life.

STEP 1
FIND THE VALUE AND TOSS THAT TRASH

"Price is what you pay. Value is what you get."
—Warren Buffett

A few weeks ago, I pulled my truck up to a house and found a big pile of green garbage bags lying next to the can. As I started to throw them into the truck, the guy who lives there walked up to me.

"I'm sorry for the mess," he said.

"You don't have to apologize," I replied. "You can throw out anything you want."

"I know. That's the problem. This was my mom's house. She has Alzheimer's and I had to move her into a home. Every time I pick up a vase or a bowl or a magazine, I ask myself, 'Does this have a great story behind it or is it junk?' Unfortunately, her memory is too far gone to help me." He looked away for a moment. "I just know I'm throwing away some of our family history. And it's killing me inside."

What he said really got me thinking. As I looked at the tons of trash that passed through my truck—all the stuff that I'm hauling out of people's lives—I realized it was there because people decided that it had no more value to them anymore. What was going on in their heads? How did they make those choices? So I started examining how my brain makes basic keep-or-toss decisions, and it didn't seem very hard: Keep the jewelry (high value) and toss the broken mug (low value).

I also realized that the same kind of thing goes on in my mind. I have a huge collection of *thoughts*, *beliefs*, and *opinions* in my head, or TBOs for short. They cover everything about me: my intelligence, my skills, my looks—the whole way I think about myself and how I fit in this crazy world. I've been collecting these feelings for years, ever since I was a little kid. I assumed that I made keep-or-toss decisions about my thoughts just like I did with my other stuff: keep the obvious ones like *I'm a pretty decent artist* and throw out the useless ones like *I'm the worst painter ever*. Then I looked a little closer at what was actually happening.

Since I've had some of these TBOs for so long, my brain naturally says, "Hey! These *must* have real value." It never even occurred to me to question whether I need them anymore, just like I never questioned why the closet was so full until I opened the door and everything fell onto my head. I'm holding on to garbage in my mind that should have been tossed a long time ago—and I'm tossing things of tremendous value that I should never have let go in the first place. Why, then, can't I toss that trash? Why do I insist on dragging it around with me year after year, long past the time when it's actually useful? It's because I don't have a working knowledge of value. That's what this chapter is going to focus on.

THE CENTRAL ROLE OF VALUE

Even though there's garbage in my truck, I don't treat my truck like garbage. That's because it's the most important tool I need to do my job and I value it very highly. I've taught myself to tune in to all the subtle ways that it works, so much so that I can tell when there's an issue with the engine or the hydraulics just by the way the truck sounds. But it wasn't always like that. When I first started out, everything was so new I couldn't see a problem until it was right on top of me.

The same thing was true growing up. When I was a kid, my folks never sat me down and said, "Here's how to tune in to your brain and figure out which thoughts to keep and which ones to toss." Instead, they put me in a sweatshirt, dropped a backpack on my shoulders, and sent me off to school with all the other kids.

What a rude awakening that was! I got into fights. I had crushes. I had friends who duped me. Without a user's manual, my little mind had no idea how to deal with all this new input, so it whipped up negative TBOs like *I must be stupid* when a teacher embarrassed me and *I'm a weakling* when I got my butt whipped by another kid. Pretty soon, all that chatter showed up in my behavior. I stopped raising my hand in class. I thought twice about where I went on the playground. It didn't matter that some teachers liked me or other kids wanted to be my friend. My brain kept latching on to the negative thoughts, as if those TBOs had the power to crush anything that tried to prove them wrong.

Now, fast-forward twenty years. When my boss asks for a volunteer to head up the truck safety program, does my hand go up? Of course not. I'm still listening to the *I must be stupid* voice in my head. When there's an opening for a route supervisor, do I apply for it? No way. I'm stupid, remember?

I know it sounds silly, but that's how I'm wired. I won't take action as a grown-up because of something that happened to me when I was a kid. I keep lugging TBOs from one period of my life to the next, even though they don't fit the person who

> I WON'T TAKE ACTION AS A GROWN-UP BECAUSE OF SOMETHING THAT HAPPENED TO ME WHEN I WAS A KID.

I am right now. It's like keeping all my clothes from the time I was born until now, even though none of them fit anymore. Seriously, how can a belief from a person I was twenty or thirty years ago be relevant to the person I am right now, today?

Having had this flash of inspiration, I realized I could do one of two things. I could let those old, outdated TBOs continue to run me, or I could find ways to take my garbageman skills and turn those TBOs to my advantage. This is where understanding value comes in. I can use it to open the door to my mind, turn on the light, and look at what's stored on my mental shelves—no different from what I do with the closet when I decide it's time to clean it out. One by one, I hold something up—a hat, a sweater, a thought, or an opinion—and ask myself, "Does this have value anymore?" If the answer is yes, it stays. If not, it goes.

Every day, I make dozens of subtle keep-or-toss decisions. All I need to do is consciously apply those skills to the stacks of TBOs I've got in my mental attic. I look at what's stored up there and I use my understanding of value to get rid of the TBOs I no longer need.

IS IT TREASURE OR IS IT TRASH?

Value can be a very slippery fish. It has a lot of different sides that can make it both powerful and difficult. The toughest lesson I learned is how easy it is to misread. Here's a great example of that.

One day, I stopped my truck in front of a double-wide trailer in a local trailer park. I knew the man who lived there was old because I'd seen him a couple of times struggling to get his can to the pick-up spot. This particular day, I noticed it wasn't out at all; the can was still under the carport. I wanted to be helpful so I ran up the driveway and dragged it to the truck, but when I flipped the lid to empty it, I noticed that it was full of dirt. Technically speaking, I wasn't supposed to dump yard debris. I hesitated for a moment, and then decided to bend the rules and do him a favor. I emptied the can, put it back under the carport, and went on my merry way.

When I showed up at his house the next week, he was standing at the curb, leaning on his cane. An oxygen tank hung over his shoulder. He signaled for me to get out of the truck.

"Are you the one…(*wheezy breath of oxygen*)…who emptied my garbage…(*wheeze*)…the last time?"

I nodded.

"Did you see…(*wheeze*)…what was inside?"

"Yeah. A bunch of dirt. I figured it was your yard debris and you put it in the wrong can."

He pointed that cane right at me like it was an extension of his finger. "Well, guess what? (*long, painful wheeze*) You figured wrong!"

It turns out the old man made his living selling fishing worms—a very special breed that people drove from miles around to buy. He needed more room to raise them so he transferred the worm farm to his garbage can. Without realizing it, I had misjudged the value of what I'd seen and had thrown away his entire livelihood.

This story goes to show how difficult value can be to work with. It's the most important tool I use to decide what's garbage and what isn't, yet what makes something valuable can be all over the board. I saw dirt in a garbage can. The old man saw a unique way to make a living. I made the wrong value call and created one heck of a mess.

The same thing applies to the TBOs running around in my head. If I don't have a clear set of criteria to determine their value, I'll have no idea which ones are helping me and which ones are tripping me up. When I say "criteria to determine their value," I mean:

- Is the TBO true?

- How do I feel once the TBO kicks in: fearful or fearless?

- When I take action on the TBO, does it help me or hold me back?

- Is this TBO new and useful, or is it a holdover from years past?

If I'm fuzzy on what makes a thought valuable, I'm going to make some boneheaded mistakes, the most obvious of which is tossing what I should keep and keeping what I should toss.

Nailing down those criteria can be tricky because what's important to me changes over time. When I was younger, I never paid attention to what I ate. Now, I see huge value in a diet that doesn't send my cholesterol through the roof. The opposite is also true. After someone stole my coin collection in high school, I got the idea that people couldn't be trusted. That TBO doesn't have much value to me now if it makes it difficult for me to make friends. If I'm not the same person I was twenty years ago (and I'm not), it's probably a bad idea to use twenty-year-old criteria to judge my current set of TBOs. I need to weigh their value based on what's important to me now, at this stage of my life.

Value is also influenced by how I'm feeling. The more connection I feel to a TBO, the more value I'm going to give it. If I like the mailman but I can't stand my next-door neighbor, which relationship am I going to value more? The same thing goes with what's inside my head. If a TBO makes me feel good, I'm going to give it a pretty high value. The problem comes when I overdo it. If I think all my TBOs are important, I'll never get rid of anything. That puts me right back at square one: too much garbage in my life.

> THE MORE CONNECTION I FEEL TO A TBO, THE MORE VALUE I'M GOING TO GIVE IT.

A quick word about TBOs. I don't want you to think that all TBOs are bad things that should be purged from your life like a disease. Some TBOs are great to have around. Let's say I formed one like *I need to be careful whom I trust* when I was a kid. That's a good thing, right? Being careful protects me by making sure I slow down before diving headfirst into an unfamiliar situation. That same TBO can be neutral, too. I may keep it around, but, given how I'm wired, I'm naturally cautious, so the TBO plays a small role in my thinking.

However, if I've morphed that belief through the years into *Never trust anyone*, that's a bad TBO and it needs to be tossed. It makes it tough to form friendships, to be open to love, and to create meaningful business partnerships. So I don't think all TBOs are trash. They can be good, neutral, or bad, depending on how that TBO makes me feel and how it influences my actions.

If you're looking for some specifics about how to create your own criteria for value, don't worry. That's coming up a little later on in this chapter. For now, just remember this: Being crystal-clear about which thoughts have value is the gateway to throwing out your trash.

ARE YOU STEPPING ON THE ACCELERATOR OR THE BRAKE?

I can't tell you how many times I want to pull my hair out when I'm on my route. I hit every red light. I can't get close enough to the cans to grab them. Cars keep cutting me off. Those are the days when I wish the trash would just throw itself into the back of the truck and I could go home.

Here's the truth. When my day starts to go sideways, I have two choices about how I can act. I can jam the accelerator to the floorboards and drive like a crazy man, or I can tap the brakes and pull my mental truck over for a while. If I choose wrong, I may end up somewhere I really don't want to be.

When I'm feeling really charged about a situation and my emotions are calling the shots, that's a *reaction* and it's a lousy time to assign value to a TBO. When my emotions are taking a back seat to calm, rational

What do you do more: react or respond? How would life be different if you did more of one and less of the other?

thinking, that's called a *response*, and my value decisions are way better when they come from here. Let me give you a great example.

I was doing my morning inspection when I heard some singing near one of the trucks. It was Tony, a driver I took under my wing a few years back. When he saw me, he stopped singing, hopped in his truck and drove away before I could say anything. A few days later we were having beers. When I told him that he had a great singing voice, his entire body stiffened and his face went cold—not the reaction I expect when I give someone a compliment.

It took me a while, but I finally wrestled out of him that he had wanted to pursue a career in musical theater when he got out of college—until his father went ballistic, told him it was a stupid idea, and threatened to pull the plug on paying for school. Tony immediately dropped the idea of being an entertainer and had never stepped foot on stage since. That was twenty-six years ago.

So what happened? As soon as his dad flew off the handle, Tony quietly created a couple of TBOs deep in his head: *A career in singing is a stupid idea* and *What my dad wants is way more important than what I want.* Without realizing it, he assigned huge value to these two beliefs. Now, two and a half decades later, they are still in control. No matter how many compliments he gets, all Tony hears is his dad chewing him out. By this point in his life, it's not his father who's stopping him anymore. It's Tony and his mental garbage.

What if he had responded instead of reacting? When his dad went off, Tony would have seen it more like a movie, as if he were watching it from a distance. He might have said to himself, "Man! Dad's all riled up about this. I wonder what that's about." Responses let you think that way.

I'm not saying that Tony won't have some strong feelings about what his dad said to him, but he would have had some breathing room around them. Would he have made the same decision not to sing? Who knows? But at least he would have had a level head to weigh his options instead of running for cover, chased by his dad's anger. Responses give you a clear picture of how much value your TBOs have. That makes it so much easier to figure out what's worth keeping and what should be on its way to the can.

SHORT-TERM AND LONG-TERM VALUE

Almost every day, I find an end table or a chair sitting at the end of the driveway that folks want me to throw away. Needless to say, these aren't family heirlooms made from solid wood. They're cheap veneer and particleboard and they don't last. That's why I inherit them instead of the grandkids. Lousy furniture is a great way to think about the two types of value: *short-term* and *long-term*.

My computer and cell phone have value, but it's not the same value as my wife's wedding ring. The friendship I just struck up with the new route supervisor is very different from the one I have with my buddy I've known since grade school. Some things have long-term value, which means they're deep and important and they'll be with me for a long time. Others have short-term value: They play a role in my life but they aren't going to be with me forever.

Longevity doesn't dictate value, though. Think about Tony. The TBOs he carried around for so many years weren't true. Singing *isn't* a stupid career and his needs were just as important as his father's. Also, if he stiffens like a board every time he gets an "atta-boy" for something positive, the TBOs he's holding on to obviously don't make him feel very good. So in this case, long-term holding doesn't equate to long-term value. Sure, those TBOs might have felt important to Tony—important enough to rule his life for decades. However, if he looked closely and applied an objective set of criteria based on who he is today, he'd see that they were garbage.

That's exactly what happened. It was tough for him to do, but he finally admitted that he'd blown off his dreams the day his dad had jumped down his throat. Sure, he made a good living as a garbageman, but what he really wanted to do with his life was to be on the stage. I asked him how long he was going to let his old trash continue to control his life. That was six months ago.

Last weekend, I took my wife and kids to a musical here in town. Want to guess who had the lead role? That's right. Tony. And the best part? There was this old guy in the back row who had a smile on his face the whole performance. It was his dad.

Sometimes, amazing things happen when you finally take out the trash.

FINDING GOLD IN THE GARBAGE

Value can turn up in places where I least expect it. My wife was telling me about a friend of hers who had just broken up with someone. This guy was bad news. He was rude, he yelled at her, and he cheated on her—twice. She felt humiliated by this guy and was painfully embarrassed because she stuck it out for so long, trying to make it work. All she wanted to do was hide under a blanket for a month and cry. That got me thinking.

> VALUE CAN TURN UP IN PLACES WHERE I LEAST EXPECT IT.

While she's licking her wounds, reacting to what happened, she's not going to see very much value in that relationship. Eventually though, that reaction will fade—and once it does, I'll bet you ten-to-one odds she's going to find some unexpected value:

- The backbone it took to finally walk away

- The guts it took to give love a shot

- How much she learned about what she won't do the next time

It doesn't matter that the relationship didn't work out. Behind every failure, mistake, and fender bender, there is usually hidden value that can be found once the reaction stops and the response kicks in. I already do that today. I may cringe from the ridiculous mistakes I make on my route (and I've had some world-class beauties in my day), but I always try to find a nugget of value so I don't slip up again.

If I widen that idea, my entire past begins to look different. Instead of beating myself up all the time, what if every wrong turn and mistake I've ever made was just a way for me to learn something? What if I said to myself that no matter how bad it might have been, whatever happened yesterday no longer controls my life?

I'll bet that would put me in a different lane.

THE VALUE SERVICE PLAN

If folks own a house and they want their trash picked up, they need to sign up for a service plan from their garbage company. They tell the company what they need hauled away and how often they want service, and I show up at their house and do the work.

The same thing goes for my inner garbage. I need a service plan that sizes up all of my old TBOs and gets rid of them if they don't have value anymore. That's the Value Service Plan: a few simple steps that help my Inner Garbageman learn the art of letting go.

1. **Create a Value Filter.**
    Earlier in this chapter, I made a list of several criteria I use to decide what's a valuable thought or belief. I'll repeat those here:

    - Is the TBO true?

    - How do I feel once the TBO kicks in: fearful or fearless?

    - When I take action on the TBO, does it help me or hold me back?

- Is this TBO new and useful, or is it a holdover from years past?

These are my core criteria—the first four questions I ask when I'm looking at a TBO and trying to judge its value. Together these form my Value Filter.

2. Run TBOs through my Value Filter.

Once I create my Value Filter, it's time to figure out which TBOs in my head are garbage. Just like the oil filter in my truck, I use my Value Filter to identify and trap any TBO that's clogging up my thinking and slowing down my performance.

My brain never stops forming TBOs. Not only am I dragging around the ones I've had since I was a kid, but new experiences are happening to me all the time. Depending on the way the situation played out, I might be taking an old TBO and creating a new variation of it, or I might be inventing an entirely new one. Whether it's ancient history or today's creation, running an old or new TBO through my Value Filter is a great way to find out if it's garbage or not.

> MY BRAIN NEVER STOPS FORMING TBOs.

Using the Value Filter is easy. Once I become aware that I'm thinking or acting in a certain way, I ask myself the core criteria questions. If I'm not getting a clear answer, I'll push myself a little more to understand what's going on. If I'm really plugged in to a certain belief or opinion, sometimes I'll add a question or two that's specific to that TBO. For example, if I'm beating myself up about the way I handle money, I'll ask myself, "Is my belief in this TBO being influenced by our current bank account balance?" Pushing myself to dig deeper like this really helps me uncover the reason why I've latched on to a specific thought that's getting me nowhere.

Using my Value Filter is not a long, drawn-out process. For most TBOs, it just takes a few seconds. Once I notice that I'm shooting myself in the foot, I usually ask, "What's that all about?" That question is like a trigger for me. I'll run the thought or the action through my Value Filter and I'll know right away if it's garbage. It felt a little weird to do this at first. I had to turn up my awareness of what I was thinking and how I was acting. Once I started though, I began using my Value Filter more and more. Now, I don't even think about it. I screen old and new thoughts all the time.

Here's the great thing about this process. There's nothing new here! I'm already using my Value Filter every time I make a keep-or-toss decision. Is the lid from the empty yogurt container useful? Nope. Throw it out. Does the newspaper I bought the day my son was born make me feel good? Yep. It has sentimental value, and I'm keeping it. All I'm doing is taking that exact same Value Filter and using it to screen the thoughts, beliefs, and opinions sitting in my head. And man, does that make it easier to find the ones that have no value!

3. Toss that trash.

When I'm throwing away physical garbage, I know it's out the door and gone. Mental garbage, on the other hand, is in my head. It's not like I can crumple it up and throw it in the nearest can. Because I can't touch it or see it, I have to be a little more deliberate when I dump it.

That's why I've created a space in my head called my *landfill*. It's the final resting place for every TBO that has no more value for me, a graveyard for useless thoughts that I don't want to haul around with me anymore. Once it goes into my landfill, I don't want to see or hear from that TBO again. (In Step 5, I'll show you how to handle a TBO if it ever blows out of the landfill and sticks to you again.)

How do I move a TBO to my landfill? Let's say I'm trying to change the oil filter on my car. After the third time the wrench has slipped and my knuckles are bleeding, I'll catch myself saying,

"You stink at auto repair." The moment that happens, I'll run the thought through my Value Filter, realize it's garbage, and tell myself to stop thinking that way. That's all it takes, a split second, and I've swept the TBO out of my mind and into my landfill.

Just to be clear, when I talk about putting an event in my landfill, I'm not getting rid of the people who were involved. Instead, I'm getting rid of the TBOs that I've made up around what happened. I'm dumping what isn't true, what keeps eating at me, and whatever is stomping on my energy, enthusiasm, and my dreams to the point where I can't move anymore. Also, I don't hang out at my landfill. Once I dump my trash there, I'm gone. Folks don't want to live with their garbage, which is why the landfill is only a place to visit, not to spend time in. When I'm torturing myself by digging around in my past, I realize that I'm dwelling in my landfill. That's when I give myself a simple order: "Get out of there. Now."

4. Keep making trips to the landfill.

I don't see many people running down the street in their slippers, chasing my truck and shouting, "Stop! I *really* want that used gum wrapper back!" For the most part, once they toss something, it's out of their minds and out of their lives for good.

Mental trash doesn't quite work like that. I may throw out a useless TBO like *No one thinks I'm smart,* only to find that it's back again two days later when I'm stumbling over a new problem. Also, I've got a huge collection of TBOs in my brain that I've collected for decades—plus, I'm adding new ones all the time. So it's a little ridiculous for me to expect that I can simply throw out all my inner trash with one wave of my mental magic wand. Whether I like it or not, there's always going to be garbage in my head.

GETTING RID OF MENTAL TRASH IS A PROCESS, NOT A ONE-TIME EVENT.

What does that mean? Getting rid of mental trash is a process, not a one-time event. It's something I need to do on a regular basis, just like emptying all the cans in my house. As I work with my Value Filter, I need to remember to keep throwing trash into my personal landfill. The more often I do it, the easier it'll be to deal with the next round of trash that comes my way.

USE CAUTION

The following pitfalls can keep me from finding the value and tossing the trash.

DON'T ASSIGN VALUE WHEN I'M MAD

I'm the first one to admit that when I'm ticked off, I make lousy decisions. It doesn't do me any good to assign value to a TBO when I'm in the middle of a full-on reaction. As our mechanic says, an engine that's cooled down is a lot easier to work on than one that's red hot and blowing steam.

So how do I avoid assigning value when I'm all worked up? The trick is *controlling* my reaction, and I've discovered three ways to do that.

1. Get ready for it. Remember how I tune in to the way my truck runs? The more I pay attention to the small stuff I hear, the more I can spot an issue long before it mushrooms into a much bigger problem. I do the same thing with what's swirling around in my head. If I pay attention to what I'm feeling and thinking and notice when I start to veer off the road, there's a good chance I can prevent a full-blown, ugly reaction.

2. Stop it. Let's say, despite giving it my best shot, my feelings take over and I'm reacting. What then? I try to zero in on that little voice in my head that's saying, "Hey! You're heading toward the cliff. Take your foot off the gas!" That voice belongs to my Inner Garbageman: the part of my brain that's objective, rational, and un-plugged from whatever's eating me.

As weird as it may sound, just noticing that I'm having a reaction is a huge step toward stopping it completely. It's like I suddenly become this person who's watching my behavior rather than being the one who's experiencing it. I see myself in some really bad viral video that will show up on YouTube, and my Inner Garbageman pokes me in the ribs and asks, "Is this *really* how you want the world to see you? Is this the face of the person you're working so hard to become?" That's usually all it takes—a split second where I can step outside of what I'm feeling, and bam! The wind is sucked right out of the reaction and I can think straight again.

3. Ride it out. Sometimes, no matter how much I've prepared and how much I try to stop it, my emotions get away from me and I can't get them under control. There I am, reacting in all my glory, swallowed up by the intensity of the moment. I know it isn't pretty. But I also know it's not going to last forever. Eventually, it'll pass and I'll calm down. So I've learned that if I can't stop the reaction, I can just ride it out to the other side. Then I can pull my truck over and decide what I should do next.

Look Under the Hood

Remember the story about the old man and the worms? No sooner had I pulled into the yard at the end of my shift than my supervisor grabbed me. "I've been on the phone with this guy and he's furious! Get back over there and make it right with him!"

As quickly as I could, I drove my car to the trailer park and knocked on the door. The old man answered, as mad as before. He let me in, pointed to the couch, and proceeded to chew me out. He was so thin and frail that I thought he was going to have a coronary as he struggled to breathe. During the entire time, his wife was sitting in a wheelchair next to him. She couldn't speak, so every time he finished a sentence, she would just point at me and scowl.

I felt terrible. This man was willing to push himself to the point of physical exhaustion in order to communicate the value of those worms to me. The more he talked, the more humbled I became. I apologized over and over again and eventually, he calmed down. He told me the story of his business: how he discovered his love for breeding worms, how he grew a huge customer base, and how he built his reputation as a worm master. I was amazed. I'd been picking up this guy's trash for years and I had no idea he was this talented.

Two hours slipped by as I talked to the old man, but I hardly noticed. Finally, I asked him the most important question: How much money would it take to get him back up and running? As soon as the words came out of my mouth, I braced myself. This guy was a legend and those worms must be worth a fortune. I figured I'd have to cancel our family vacation. And forget about the new TV I had promised the kids. Man, my wife was going to kill me...

The old man thought for a moment. "Pay for everything? Start to finish?"

I nodded.

"What I think it's worth?"

"Yeah."

He turned to his wife, who nodded at him. Clearly, they had discussed this before I had arrived. The old man leaned forward, a stern and serious look on his face.

"Forty bucks, son. And not a *penny* less."

Surprised? So was I. The more I thought about that, the more I began to pick out some huge lessons, all under the banner of "look under the hood."

First, it's so easy to classify something as garbage and blow it off—then find out later that it's incredibly important. Once, I dismissed a new guy I met at work as inconsequential—until I found out later that he was our new general manager. Not a good way to start our working relationship, was it?

Second, I should never assume that everyone's assessment of value matches mine. I figured the old man's worms were worth hundreds, maybe even thousands of dollars. To him, they were worth forty bucks. What I learned is that folks see value in their own way—and that may not match what I think or believe.

Finally, I realized that forty bucks was a lot more money to the old man than it was to me. I need to respect other people and where they are in their lives, financially and emotionally, if I want to avoid creating a mess.

Here's the bottom line of looking under the hood: Until I have all the facts, it's best for me to hang back, go slow, and not jump to any hasty conclusions.

Watch Out for the Flashy Paint Job

When our mechanic is looking over a used truck to see if the company should buy it, the shiny body and the steam-cleaned engine never sucker him in. He inspects every inch before deciding how much value he sees.

I'm working on getting that same skill for myself. I cringe at the times when I've been attracted by the promise of a friendship, and then find out that the other person had a hidden agenda. Or the times when one TBO is lurking behind another one, like when I think I'm lousy at public speaking, but I realize later that I'm actually scared to death of crowds.

When have you been fooled by a façade? Looking back on the experience, were there any warning signs that you missed?

I've also noticed that value can trick me into thinking a TBO is world-class when it's actually garbage. Wouldn't it be great if everything had a warning sticker on it? I wish I could go into a store and find a label that says, CAUTION! ONE-THIRD OF THE MATERIALS USED TO MAKE THIS SOFA IS PURE GARBAGE. Same thing with people. How much easier would life be if we each had a sign hanging around our neck: WARNING! ONE-FOURTH OF THE TIME AND TWO-THIRDS OF THE ENERGY YOU SPEND ON THIS PERSON WILL BE TOTALLY WASTED. What a timesaver that would be!

If I don't want to get duped by a flashy paint job, I need be more like a mechanic: Look under the hood and see what's really going on.

USE MY TEAM WISELY

When it's all said and done, I have to take out my own mental trash. No one else can do that for me. At the same time, garbage can get pretty heavy, so it's nice to have a little help every once in a while, especially with the big stuff. That's when talking to my team helps: friends, people I work with, a counselor. They make me look at all the angles. They give me feedback. They help me step away and see things as they are. I've learned that talking about value out loud always sounds different from the way it plays out in my head—and that can really help when I'm making keep-or-toss decisions.

> I HAVE TO TAKE OUT MY OWN MENTAL TRASH. NO ONE ELSE CAN DO THAT FOR ME.

You should see me during some of these talks. I'll be fighting tooth and nail to defend some old, broken-down TBO that I'm being told to my face is about as helpful as a flat tire. So I have three rules when I'm talking to someone on my team: (1) Listen to what's being said, even if I don't like it, (2) don't dump so much garbage that I bury the other person in my story, and (3) keep a lid on anything I shouldn't be sharing. The last thing I want is to have my personal garbage blowing around the neighborhood.

DON'T BE TRIGGER-HAPPY

As I'm trying to keep my can empty, sometimes the most random thing can bring back old TBOs that I thought had long since been thrown away.

We were at a company lunch last week and I noticed halfway through that Judy, one of the customer service reps, had walked out of the room. I found her sitting alone in the lobby.

It turns out that the folks at her table were talking about marriage: how long they'd been together and how happy they were. She had left the lunch because she found herself second-guessing a date she had had a few weeks back—a terrible evening out with a guy who talked about nothing but himself the entire night.

"These crazy thoughts started crossing my mind," Judy said. "Maybe he wasn't *that* bad. Maybe I was too quiet. What if no one else comes along?" She threw her hands in the air. "I know in my gut that this guy is a lousy match for me, yet I found myself wanting to call him again. What's wrong with me?"

I told her absolutely nothing was wrong because I've done the same thing a million times myself. An event sets me off and, before I know what hits me, my mind has grabbed a shovel and is furiously digging up the garbage from my past. I call those events Trash Triggers™: a person, circumstance, or situation that causes me to change a value decision that I already made.

Anything can be a Trash Trigger: a smell, a sunset, a song, or a life event like the anniversary of a loved one's death. They create a false sense of urgency by making me think that I have to act *now*, before it's too late! That can create a huge mess, especially when the best thing is to sit on my hands and do nothing at all.

Start thinking about the Trash Triggers that get you every time. What can you do to stop them?

I manage Trash Triggers the same way as I manage my Value Filter: by being aware that they're there and that they can make me do weird things if I'm not careful. In Judy's case, when her finger was hovering over the Send button, ready to text this guy again, she forced herself to think twice. That's a great way to step in front of a Trash Trigger: discipline, a half-second pause, and thinking about the consequences of acting on impulse. When I put those three things together, I can usually stop a Trash Trigger from getting me into much trouble.

TAKING IT TO THE STREET

SUMMARY: FIND THE VALUE AND TOSS THAT TRASH

The first step in getting rid of the trash in my mind is to realize which thoughts, beliefs, and opinions are actually mental garbage. To help me figure that out, I use the same piece of reasoning that lets me decide what is physical garbage: determine its value. Whether I've had a thought for a while or a fresh one has just popped into my head, determining its value helps me quickly sort out whether the TBO is worth keeping or whether I should toss it.

To do this, I create a Value Filter: a list of criteria I've created that helps me flesh out the amount of value a TBO may have. Is this TBO true? Is it moving me forward or keeping me anchored in my past? Then, I run a specific TBO that's been bothering me through my Value Filter. If it turns out that it's garbage and not worth keeping anymore, I throw the TBO into my landfill and move on.

Since I already use a Value Filter to make keep-or-toss decisions about physical garbage, all I need to do is widen that Value Filter to include the contents of my mind. That means paying a little closer attention to what I'm thinking about and how I'm acting. Once I start running that through my Value Filter, it becomes easier to pick out the garbage and get rid of it. I watch out for some of value's pitfalls by not taking value in others for granted, not getting caught up in value's façades, and looking out for Trash Triggers.

Value can be a little tricky to work with. It changes all the time, depending on the situation I'm in and the TBO that I'm looking at. Plus, value is influenced by how I feel. If I'm in the middle of a heavy-duty reaction, I'll get a totally different read on value than if I'm level-headed and calm. Knowing this, my Value Filter can compensate for these fluctuations, which means I can throw out what I don't need and keep my mind open to the things I really want to accomplish in my life.

EXERCISES

1. I've defined value from the point of view of the garbageman. Based on what you've read and your own personal experience, what is your definition of value?

_____

_____

_____

_____

_____

_____

2. Create your own Value Filter. What questions would help you decide if a TBO has any value? You can use the Value Filter questions in this chapter as a starting point, or you can make up your own.

_____

_____

_____

_____

_____

_____

3. Choose a thought, belief, or opinion that's in your mind. It can be a new one that you just formed or one that you've carried for years. Run it through your Value Filter. Is it worth keeping, or is it garbage?

    _____

    _____

4. If the TBO is garbage, write down the method you think would best help you get rid of it. When you're done, throw the TBO out of your mind.

    _____

    _____

    _____

    _____

    _____

5. Do you think this TBO will come back in your mind again? If so, list the Trash Triggers that might cause it to return. If not, write down at least three Trash Triggers that you do know about that cause old garbage to reappear.

    _____

    _____

    _____

    _____

    _____

STEP 2
KEEP IT EMPTY

"The wisdom of life consists of the elimination of nonessentials."
—Lin Yutang

When I was a kid, my mom would buy me shoes that were just a little too big so I'd have room to grow into them. When I helped my dad plant new trees in the backyard, he would leave a lot of space between them so they'd have room to grow. When I started third grade, my parents moved us to a new house because they said we all needed the extra room.

I've heard this my whole life: Everything needs empty space to grow. Now, growth isn't something that happens just once and then stops. It's going on all the time: in my body, in my mind, in my spiritual life, and in my job. If I don't keep creating emptiness in all of those areas, I'm going to fill up whatever open space I have left. And that's either going to slow down my growth or stop it altogether.

So what's the best way to keep creating the empty space that I need? *Get rid of the clutter that wants to fill it up*. And that's exactly what I do as a garbageman: haul away all the candy wrappers and broken mugs and burned-out light bulbs that clutter up people's lives. When I clear that stuff away and hand them back an empty garbage can, they have the room they need to keep growing.

That same concept applies to the contents of my head. I'm always coming across new ideas and having new experiences. If I don't get rid of my mental trash, I end up cluttering my mind until I'm trapped by my past and all the problems and issues that I've never cleaned out of my life. Anything new gets lost in all that old garbage, and I keep repeating the same patterns over and over again. And if I want to plan a new direction for myself? Forget about it. When my mind is dominated by thoughts, beliefs, and opinions from my past, there's no room for me to grow into that new person.

In Step 1, I talked about how to recognize mental trash and how to throw it out. When I do that, I create a space for new thoughts, a gap that I call *emptiness*. That space in my mind is absolutely essential to a healthy life. It's the mental breathing room I need to see new opportunities, create big new dreams for myself, and stretch into places that I've never been. And I can't get access to it if my head is crammed full with old garbage from my past.

If I've learned one thing about mental trash, it's that the emptiness that comes after dumping it is one of the most powerful and life-changing forces I've ever encountered. That's what I'm going to talk about in this chapter, because once I learned how to harness emptiness, my life was never the same again.

WHAT IS EMPTINESS?

Imagine that you just walked in the front door of a dance studio. What do you see? A big, empty space. Room to move. Room to create. Room for the art to show up.

Now think about other places like that: a huge cathedral, an art gallery, an old palace you may have visited overseas. People sometimes call these buildings spacious. To me, that's just another word for emptiness. It's the openness and elbow room that make these buildings so amazing.

Once I started thinking about emptiness, I began seeing it everywhere. Music has it (the space between notes to create its rhythm). Freeways have it (the space between cars). Every sentence in this book has it (suremakesreadingmucheasier!). You know what the difference is between a day when I'm totally frazzled and a day when I can think straight? It's usually an empty mind or an empty calendar.

If I think about it, the world is actually a balance between what is and what isn't, between emptiness and "somethingness." Just like those days when I'm running in a hundred different directions, it's only when I fill up all my empty space that my balance gets thrown off and I usually get myself into trouble. I face this every day with my truck. There's only so much garbage I can pack in there. If I don't empty it when it's full, I run the risk of damaging it—or possibly even tipping it over.

This idea of emptiness is nothing new. I remember reading about it in school when I studied the Mayans and the Native Americans. These days, I hear about naturopaths, energy healers, and folks who practice feng shui. Some of my buddies write these people off as being "way out there." I think they're right. These people are way out there—right in the middle of a big field of emptiness. And they're all hammering home the same message: Get rid of what you don't need and put it in your landfill, and life will feel a whole lot lighter.

WHY EMPTINESS IS HARD TO WORK WITH

After ten years in the same house, I decided to redesign the backyard. I walked outside, looked around, then closed my eyes and tried to imagine that the whole space was empty. Then I started to fill it with plants, trellises, and decks. I can't plan a new beginning if I'm still boxed in by the clutter of the past.

My mind works the exact same way. If I'm always going back to the same set of TBOs to make my choices and decisions, how in the world can I come up with anything new? I *need* emptiness to think, to clear my mental decks of all those TBOs that keep pounding on me for attention.

> I NEED EMPTINESS TO THINK, TO CLEAR MY MENTAL DECKS.

The trouble is that I live in a physical world. My attention goes to what I can touch or see, not to what isn't there. It's like someone telling me that the best part of a donut is the hole in the middle. Not only does that not make sense, it's also a little weird.

But here's the reality. The secret to building anything—a new house or a new life—is the way I treat emptiness. If I toss an old, outdated TBO into my landfill and the emptiness makes me jittery and uncomfortable, my brain may try to fill that emptiness with another thought similar to what I just threw out. And guess what that could get me? The same frustrating results, over and over again.

Take my wife, for example. She had it really tough when she was a kid. Her dad was like a drill sergeant and criticized her the second she made a mistake. To make matters worse, her mom was afraid of her dad, so she hardly stood up for my wife when she got in trouble. As a result, my wife created some very specific TBOs about love, doozies like *I expect to be treated poorly* and *Love does not mean affection.*

So she started dating. And who do you think she chose? Guys who picked on everything she did. Guys who badmouthed her, tore her down, and treated her lousy. It's not like she was doing this on purpose. But in her mind, this was the way love was supposed to be, all thanks to a pile of negative TBOs she had created when she was a kid and never circled back to throw out.

Now I'm no saint, but I know how to treat a woman I care about. And I was *nuts* about my wife after we met. At first, she had no idea what to do with me! She figured if a guy was treating her this nicely, he must be up to something, so she totally rejected me. But I'm pretty persistent when I want to be and eventually she came around—but only after she got rid of her old TBOs about what kind of guy she thought she deserved. Once she did that, the emptiness in her thinking left room for something new to show up—me. Which makes me the luckiest guy in the world. Now do you see why I'm such a big fan of emptiness?

WHY WE DON'T LIKE EMPTINESS

It took me a while to wrap my head around the idea of appreciating what's not there. I realized that if I wanted to master the idea of emptiness, I'd first have to understand why I wanted to fill it up in the first place.

You've probably heard the old expression "Nature abhors a vacuum." It's really true. Give me a warm beach and a cold beer and I can clear my head in no time. But in the middle of a crazy, jam-packed workday? Or on a weekend when I've got a million errands to do and I'm driving the kids all over creation? I don't know about you, but when I'm like that, clearing my head is impossible. My TBOs feel like they're in full control of my sanity, and let me tell you, that's not a pretty sight.

When my mind is swirling in garbage, the last thing it wants to do is throw out TBOs and hang out in the vacuum that's left behind. It knows that emptiness can be brutally uncomfortable. Instead, it clings to what it knows and it won't give it up. Since we were just talking about dating, think about this. You've probably heard that the

What's the balance between getting and getting rid of in your life?

STEP 2: KEEP IT EMPTY   47

worst thing you can do after breaking up with someone is to jump right into another relationship—the proverbial "from the frying pan into the fire" syndrome. It's much better to take some time to get over what happened, then start dating again.

The same thing is true with inner trash. By the time I've grabbed my mental crowbar and pried loose decades of *I can't* and *I'm not good enough,* all that emptiness I've created is going to feel really strange. My gut instinct is to fill that emptiness with the first thought that comes along, especially if it looks and feels familiar. Though I know that's the last thing I should do, my stubborn brain wants to fill that vacuum as quickly as possible. It's a really hard urge to resist.

When Hurricane Isaac barreled down on New Orleans in the summer of 2012, the local radio station interviewed a shrimp boat captain about his preparations. He had moved his boat and his family far inland, where he planned to wait out the storm. "What about your house? Your car?" the reporter asked. Having lost everything he owned seven years earlier during Hurricane Katrina, the captain replied that the family didn't have much anymore. They lived in a trailer instead of a house and they had less stuff around them. "The sea gives us life," he said, "and sometimes it takes things away as its price."

Talk about wisdom! This humble shrimp boat captain taught himself to place a really high value on *getting rid of,* both physically and mentally. He filled the emptiness created by Katrina with a deep acceptance of what he couldn't control. The result? He grew much closer to his family and he achieved a sense of peace inside. That's a noble, Zen-like way to reuse emptiness.

To better appreciate emptiness, I had to dump the traditional way I defined that word. Here's what I get when I Google it: doing without, deprivation, suffering, a feeling of being alone, cut off, and unfulfilled. Not a very uplifting word, is it?

Well, consider this. You're two chapters into a book about a garbageman. If you've made it this far, you're probably starting to rewrite your ideas about who this guy is and what he can do for you. Try doing the same thing with emptiness: Turn your idea of what you think it is on its head. Look, if I can find wisdom in trash, you can find wisdom in emptiness. In fact, it's emptiness itself—the freedom to think in a new and different way—that lets you see emptiness in a whole new light. That's a pretty cool brain-twister, isn't it?

THE MYTH OF COLLECTING

When it comes to wanting the next shiny thing, I'm as guilty as anyone. I get a strong hit about something in the store or I read about a new idea, and *bam!* I automatically click into *Gotta get that!* mode. And why not? New is cool! New is fresh! New gets my blood pumping! Our hauling operation is exactly the same. Whenever we get a new garbage truck, everyone starts sucking up to the route supervisor for a shot at driving it.

There's only one problem. New always becomes old. Eventually, the excitement fades and the shine wears off. Things don't work out the way I expected, so my wandering brain pushes my attention to the next new thing. The problem is that I never take the time to dump the emotional garbage that's left behind—feelings like jealousy and disappointment, or my failure to communicate. Guess what happens? The garbage takes over again. I react the same way, I take the same actions, and I feel all the same feelings. No wonder I get so frustrated. There's so much *old* garbage in my way that there's no room for anything *new* to appear!

This gets really tricky when I think about the golden rule of garbage: For everything I get, I give something up. When I buy a couch

| FOR EVERYTHING I GET, I GIVE UP SOMETHING. |

or a candy bar, I give up money. When I tell myself that I'm not good enough or smart enough, I give up confidence and happiness. It's like my mind is wired backward. It holds onto unhealthy TBOs that shred my self-esteem and throws out useful TBOs that build it up. Combine that with the moth-to-the-flame attraction I have for new things and it's no wonder my life skids out of control sometimes.

You know the worst thing I can do? Tell myself that all I need is *one more thing* and I'll finally be happy. The problem with that is my mind is never satisfied. It always **MY MIND WANTS MORE BECAUSE THAT'S HOW IT'S BEEN TRAINED.** wants more because that's how it's been trained. I may create emptiness by throwing out an old TBO, but my first instinct is to scan all the thoughts and opinions passing through my head and grab the first one that looks, feels, and smells like what I just tossed. Without realizing it, I'm right back where I started, with the same old garbage at the controls. If I'm going to create something new for myself, I need to put the brakes on collecting and do a whole lot more emptying.

THE POWER OF EMPTINESS

Our garage had been a total mess for so long, I think the car would have had a heart attack if I had parked it inside. Bags everywhere. Stuff crammed in every corner. When I tripped while trying to slither past a stack of boxes, I had finally had enough. I grabbed the family and we spent a long Saturday cleaning the place out.

I was shocked at how easy it was to get rid of all that junk! Everyone agreed on a simple Value Filter rule: If we hadn't used it, touched it, or thought about it in the past six months, it was gone. And here's the strange part. I wasn't prepared for the radical difference in how empty the garage looked after we finished. It was like the day we moved in! You could get to the shelves again. You could find things. I could open the freezer door without taking my life into my hands. Now, when I step foot in the garage, I smile instead of cringing. It's like someone remodeled our house—for free!

It wasn't long before I realized that dumping negative TBOs could do the same thing for my mind. I'd have freedom from all their limitations and restrictions. I'd have the opportunity to fill the emptiness with something totally new. I'd have the excitement of not knowing what to expect. I tried to imagine myself being full of emptiness, like being stuffed after a great meal. I know it's a play on words—being full of emptiness—but it's the perfect way to describe it.

I realized that if I crave emptiness, it makes getting rid of garbage so much easier. Once I started thinking and acting differently, I began hunting down old, outdated TBOs with a vengeance. My tolerance for all that old thinking went to zero. A thought would pop into my head and I would find myself asking, "Why am I hanging on to this?" The more I tuned my brain to notice emptiness, the easier it was to work with it.

That brings me back to my garage. Now that it's cleaned out, I'm going to be very careful not to let it fill up like that ever again. Same thing with the emptiness in my mind. After all the work I'm putting in to clean out all that old stuff, you can bet that I'm going to guard that emptiness like a pit bull. Just like my kids would never write a report on current affairs using a twenty-year-old encyclopedia, using old TBOs to run my life doesn't make sense to me anymore. So it's out with the old TBOs. And the emptiness I create? It stays wide open and well guarded until I decide what new thought, belief, or opinion I'm going to fill it with.

THE EMPTY AND RETURN ACTION PLAN

Ever seen one of those huge construction debris containers? There's a phrase we use when we take them to the landfill, dump them, and bring them back to the customer: empty and return. It's also a great phrase for an emptiness action plan because it can have two very powerful meanings:

- If I put a huge value on emptiness, I'll get a huge return on my investment.

- Emptiness (the space I open up in my mind when I toss my emotional garbage into my landfill) can be the path to return me to the life I really want.

1. Go clean something—outside.

When I need to practice emptiness, the first thing I do is find something in my life that needs to be cleaned out: a file cabinet in my home office, the glove compartment in my car, or the downstairs coat closet. It doesn't matter what it is, so long as it's something I use all the time. Why is this important?

- It's an easy way to practice using my Value Filter.

- It forces me to toss stuff that I don't need anymore.

- It creates the habit of emptying trash that lives outside of the garbage can.

- I get that awesome shock every time I see the newly cleaned space. That's why I make it an area I see every day, so I get a little reward for the hard work I put in *and* a reminder to keep the emptiness clean until the right things come along to fill it.

2. Go clean something—inside.

Once I've taken care of an area on the outside, I like to follow it up with a cleanup project on the inside. I hunt down an unhelpful TBO that's been dogging me for a long time—and I get rid of it by putting it in my landfill. To do that, I try to remember the first time I created it, as well as the reason why. Then, I ask myself why I'm still using it after all this time. What effect has it had on me over the years? What have I gained? What have I lost?

Then, I imagine myself throwing out that TBO. I don't have a set way I do that. I just go with whatever hits me. Sometimes, I pretend I'm throwing it into a garbage can. Or I imagine it in the back of my truck. Other times, I literally write it down on a piece of paper and burn it. The method doesn't matter. All that's important is that I get it out of my head.

Next, I focus on the emptiness that's left in its place. I try to imagine what it's like to be free from that old TBO's influence. I try to see how the way I look at life has been changed now that it's gone. Staring straight into that emptiness, I think about what I might do now that I'm rid of that old way of thinking.

That's the root of getting rid of internal garbage. The more contrast there is between the me *with* the unhelpful TBO and the me *without* it, the better my chances are that I won't fill the emptiness with the same old trash. I want the mental equivalent of that clean garage, including the jolt of pleasure when I see the difference between the old and the new me.

3. Find eight minutes of emptiness.

This action item is pretty easy to implement: Find eight minutes of emptiness every day.

I'm talking the length of three songs or a decent coffee break. That's all. Instead of checking CNN or Facebook, I tell my brain to focus on emptiness: where it shows up in my life, how different I feel when I create it, and how I can fill my jam-packed mind with more of it.

How do I do this? Sometimes, I go for a walk during my morning or afternoon break and think about nothing but emptiness. Or I'll write down a TBO and scribble out some thoughts about what life would look like if I tossed it. Other times, I just close my eyes, focus on my breathing, and think about life without TBOs that knock me down. Let me tell you something. Those eight minutes have really changed me.

4. **Get used to the discomfort of emptiness.**

My garbage truck is no limousine. It's a gritty, hard-working machine made up of rubber, metal, and hydraulics. The cab can be freezing cold in the winter and brutally hot in the summer, and it's not a very comfortable rig to drive. I remember when I first started this job. I'd climb out of that truck at the end of my route feeling like I'd just gone ten rounds in a boxing ring. As time wore on though, my muscles adapted and the soreness faded. It's like my body got used to being knocked around, and it wasn't a big deal anymore.

The same thing happened to me when I began to toss my mental garbage into my landfill. At first, it was really uncomfortable. I was so used to putting myself down or telling myself that I had no skills that I wasn't sure what to think once I started to throw that garbage out. My head just couldn't deal with that hole I'd just created, so it kicked into overtime, trying to refill itself with the same old garbage that I had just tossed.

It was no great surprise that I was doing this. I've been collecting and holding trash for years. It's not like I can flick a mental switch and make it all go away. Take the first car I bought when I got out of college—a sky blue VW Bug. In my usual overzealous fashion, I read a stack of repair manuals and completely rebuilt it from the chassis up. Over time, that little VW became like a best friend. I loved every mile I put on it.

Then, I moved to Arizona. The Bug had no air-conditioning and I was roasting, so I sold it and bought a boring, four-door sedan because it could keep me cool. I regretted it the moment I handed over the keys. The emptiness I felt from the loss of that old car ate me alive. When I couldn't stand it anymore, I went out on a hot Saturday morning and scoured every used car lot until I found another sky blue VW Bug.

It didn't take me long to realize the mistake I had made. This wasn't my old car. Nothing about it was the same—including that "old friend" feeling I used to have. A few weeks after I bought it, I sold it and lost about five hundred bucks in the process.

> I NEED TO GET USED TO THE DISCOMFORT OF EMPTINESS.

Here's what I learned: I need to get used to the discomfort of emptiness. Eventually, I'll figure out what to fill it with. Instead of fighting the awkwardness, just relax into it. Once I started doing that, getting rid of my mental trash became a pleasure, not a chore.

5. Guard the Empty Zone.

As soon as I got used to the discomfort of emptiness, it was time to take the next step: Guard it until the right TBOs come along.

To do this, I gave a name to the open space I created: the Empty Zone™. In my mind, I put a big fence around it. I heard the gate lock in place. I took up my position in front and jealously protected it, filling that Empty Zone only with thoughts, beliefs, and opinions that were 100 percent aligned with the new direction I wanted to head in (more on this in the next chapter). *Nothing else gets in.* If a familiar trashy thought shows up, I let the dogs off the leash and chase it away.

Mostly, I remind myself that I'm building a brand new life. Old garbage has no place in it anymore.

USE CAUTION

If I want to avoid making mistakes when I'm working with emptiness, I need to watch out for these four trouble spots.

Don't Go Overboard

As I guard my empty space, I have to remember not to go overboard. My goal is not to eradicate every single thought that crosses my mind in an attempt to keep all my Empty Zones from filling up. They are empty on a temporary basis only. I want to hold them open until the *right* thoughts show up—and no longer. If a thought wants to drag me back to my old self, *that's* the one I want to block—not everything in my path.

DON'T UNDERESTIMATE

I get so used to bringing "stuff" into my life that I underestimate my ability to do without. For example, I don't think twice about using portable toilets. I hop in and out of those things all the time even though they're not exactly the most appealing places to take care of business. Same thing with camping or figuring out how to cook when the power goes out. When I shift my thinking, I can be pretty adaptable.

You probably know what I'm going to say next: You can do the same thing with the thoughts in your head. At the same time, I also understand that it's never as easy as it seems. Some of your TBOs are really complicated. They were formed during some painful times in your life, and their grip on you is very real. I'm not suggesting for a minute that you can simply toss them aside by reading a few pages in a book.

However, these old beliefs and opinions don't have to run your life anymore. No matter how big and nasty they may be, you're equally capable of drawing a line in the sand and ordering them out of the driver's seat. All it takes is practice, discipline, and a rock-solid, unshakable belief in the person you say you want to be. So don't sell yourself short! Think about what you've overcome in your life. That's what you can draw on when your journey hits a speed bump. And believe me, that will get you through to the other side.

THE SMALL STUFF COUNTS TOO

When I first began experimenting with tossing my inner garbage, I thought that everything I should get rid of had to be linked to one of my huge, life-altering events. Then I realized that most of my mental chatter is actually made up of small stuff that needs some mental housecleaning, too.

I'm not saying that the big stuff didn't play a major role in getting me to the place I'm at today. I know it did. At the same time though, it's a little too simplistic for me to point to those events and say, "They are the *only* reasons why I do the crazy stuff I do." A ship doesn't reach its destination by making two or three big turns. It's the hundreds of small course corrections along the way that eventually get it into the dock. Same with me. I'm way more than a handful of big events. I'm the result of thousands of tiny decisions I've made throughout my life. Getting rid of the garbage that came from those can make all the difference.

What small stuff shaped the person you are today?

Our friend Janelle is a perfect example of this. She has an adorable four-year-old daughter who, for the most part, is a pretty reasonable kid. However, we began to notice that every time she came over to visit with her mom, she was wearing the same pink dress. It was cute at first, but after a couple of months, that thing was looking pretty ratty. When we asked Janelle about this, she just smiled and shook her head.

"I tried to get her to change into something else," she told us, "but she just dug in her heels. Nothing worked: threats, punishments, promises of treats and special privileges. She flat-out refused to take off that dress."

Then Janelle told us something interesting. She asked herself why it was driving her nuts that her daughter wouldn't change. And the answers surprised her. She didn't want people to think she'd lost control of her own kid. She was afraid everyone would think she was a bad mom if her child looked like a wreck. She felt like she was in a power struggle and didn't know how to stop it. That's when Janelle realized that those thoughts were mostly garbage and all her kid wanted to do was to wear her favorite dress. So she dumped those thoughts and stopped worrying about that little pink dress. Sure enough, when the fuss stopped, her daughter got tired of it and off it came.

Small thing, real world results. A dress may not change the course of your life. But getting rid of the trash surrounding it can definitely move you in a different direction.

BELIEVE IN YOUR VISION

Before I became a garbage truck driver, I worked for a little company on the other side of town. They were growing fast and important customers started to visit, so the company tightened its dress code. You had to start looking nice so they would make a good impression.

There was a woman named Donna who worked in marketing. She always talked about wanting to be the head of the department. But she kept wearing tie-dye skirts and flip-flops to work. Her manager told her a bunch of times to stick to the new dress code, but she wouldn't listen. Eventually, the company had no choice but to fire her.

When she was let go, I realized that saying I want something to change isn't enough. It has to get into my blood and I have to truly crave it. At the end of the day, Donna wasn't cut out to be a suited-up executive because she wasn't truly committed to becoming that kind of an employee. If I do the same thing—say, I want to create emptiness and change my life—but I don't really believe in the concept, guess what happens? The garbage hangs on. And that's the road to disappointment and regret.

If I want emptiness, I have to believe in it. Then, I have to do the work it takes to create it: Start throwing out my old trash into my landfill. It doesn't matter that I'm not sure what to fill it with or that I'm not used to the emptiness. In the old days, those were excuses. Now, they're just things I have to learn. All that matters is that I stay committed to my mission: getting rid of the garbage that's in my way.

TAKING IT TO THE STREET

SUMMARY: KEEP IT EMPTY

The phrase "get rid of your garbage" means dumping all of the old habits that are stopping me from having the life I really want. It's tossing out all the thoughts, beliefs, and opinions that keep limiting me and holding me back. It's recognizing that my mental garbage is nothing more than outdated behaviors that I picked up when I was a kid and never bothered to get rid of as an adult. It literally means tossing a part of who I am and replacing it with the person I am trying to become.

When I get rid of garbage by putting it in my landfill, I open up empty space in my mind—an Empty Zone that I'll eventually fill with new, more helpful TBOs that line up with the person I want to be. Emptiness is temporarily uncharted territory where I'm creating a whole new life for myself. It's the place where positive replaces negative, where beliefs and opinions that shoot me in the foot are swept away and a garbage-free Empty Zone is created.

Keeping that space open can be really tough. My mind doesn't like the unknown. As soon as I throw out an old belief or opinion, it wants to fill that void as quickly as possible with another TBO that looks and feels the same. So what if it's negative or self-defeating? It's familiar—and my brain will always reach for what it knows. It's used to *getting*, not *getting rid of*, so its first reflex is to grab on to what's safe and never let go.

My job is to draw a line in the sand and not allow that old stuff to fill up the emptiness I just created. Emptiness lets me say, "I'm *done* with this garbage! I don't care how uncomfortable all that open space in my brain may feel. Once I throw out the trash, I'm only going to fill it with thoughts, beliefs, and opinions that support the new vision I have for myself. And I'm going to guard this Empty Zone and keep it open until those new, useful TBOs come along."

Once I change my mindset like this, new opportunities seem to open up left and right. That's not chance or coincidence. It's the ability to see all the places that the old trash used to block. That's why emptiness is so powerful. It unhooks me from the old life I used to lead and lets me turn my focus to the life I want to build.

EXERCISES

1. **Name the top five events (positive or negative) that shaped your life and the person you are today.**

_____

_____

_____

_____

_____

2. **Write down the top five pieces of emotional garbage that you're carrying with you today and would like to give up. (Focus on thoughts, beliefs, or opinions, not events.)**

_____

_____

_____

_____

_____

3. **If you dumped the emotional garbage you just wrote down, what would you bring into your life in its place?**

_____

_____

_____

_____

_____

4. **What automatic behaviors do you have that you need to throw away to make that change happen?**

_____

_____

_____

_____

_____

5. **What role do you think emptiness can play in your life?**

_____

_____

_____

_____

_____

6. Imagine a seesaw in your mind. On one end is *getting*. On the other end is *getting rid of*. Is the seesaw even? Is it tipped in one direction or another? Draw a picture of it, labeling each end.

_____

7. What specific steps would you need to make in order to restore balance between *getting* and *getting rid of?*

_____

_____

_____

_____

_____

8. Look back at the pieces of emotional garbage you listed and choose one. Write down a new thought, belief, or opinion that you'd use to fill the emptiness.

_____

_____

_____

_____

_____

STEP 3
CREATE YOUR ROUTE

---

*"By persisting in your path,
though you forfeit the little, you gain the great."*
—*Ralph Waldo Emerson*

My dad was an amazing man.

Everything he did had a plan to it. He knew he wanted to serve in the army. He knew he wanted to get married and start a family. He knew what kind of job he wanted. And when we kids grew up and left the house, he knew the kind of retirement he wanted with my mother. He was always setting goals and creating a methodical path to reach them.

He did all of this planning for each stage of his life: a soldier, a young father, or a middle-aged shop foreman. Every one of these stages took him in a different direction, but never to some random place. It's not that my dad was rigid or lacked spontaneity. He was one of the most fun, adventurous people I've ever met. What impressed me about him was that he always knew where he was going and what he was trying to accomplish.

Now, compare that to me. When I was young, I didn't have a clue what I wanted. I'd get a vague idea of a direction, follow it for a while, and then wander off somewhere else. I was so unfocused that I once had a girlfriend break up with me because of it. "How can I take you seriously?" she told me. "You're like a plastic cup blowing around an empty parking lot."

It wasn't until I became a garbageman that I began to understand how my dad had organized his life—and what was missing from mine. When I climb into my truck in the morning and leave the yard, I don't just drive around town and pick up any garbage can I find. I follow a route: a specific set of houses or businesses that I have to take care of that day. There are some major benefits to having a route: a sense of direction and purpose, clarity as to what I have to get done, and the ability to measure my progress. Routes are the bread and butter of what I do.

That's also why my dad was so successful. He used routes all the time. When he wanted to get married, he planned a way to meet women. When he wanted to become a machinist, he planned his apprenticeship. No chaos. No drama. Just a focused person who knew what he wanted and what he had to do to get it.

In the last chapter, I talked about the Empty Zones that I create after I toss my mental trash. The last thing I want to do is fill those back up with more garbage. Well, if I know what I want in each key area of my life, any TBO that doesn't match what I want is trash—and I'm not letting garbage into my head anymore. My days of blowing around are over. That's what I'm going to cover in this chapter: how to create a route so I never get off course again.

NOTHING STAYS THE SAME

I don't know about you, but it seems like my life never stays the same. I finally get used to things being a certain way, and *bam!* I turn around and they've changed. I look at where I am and I can see the road that brought me here, but half the time, it feels like I was just along for the ride.

That began to bother me. When I'm at work, I'm running a carefully designed route. I know exactly where I'm going and I know exactly what I have to pick up, right down to the serial number of the can. By paying attention to the details, I got so good at my route I was able to shave hours off how long it took me to finish it. So I asked myself a simple question: With those kinds of skills, why was I leaving the rest of my life to chance?

Here's the embarrassing truth. Even though I work with routes in my job, it never even occurred to me to create them for my personal life. And if that weren't enough, there are all these other tools I use to get me where I want to go. I use Google to find websites. I use the maps on my phone and the GPS in my car to get me to a restaurant. There I was, surrounded by all these route-based tools, and I still was oblivious to the fact that the same idea could help me set a direction for my life.

I'll tell you what finally pushed it over for me. My wife heard that a national chain wanted to build a huge superstore in our neighborhood and she was very unhappy. She formed a little resistance group and recruited a few volunteers. As soon as the local newspaper caught wind of what was happening, a reporter

Does your life feel like it has direction and purpose?

phoned her and asked why her group was against the development. I was standing in the room when she answered: There were traffic issues, the noise—one reason after another. Then, she dropped the big one: She said that she didn't think this kind of store fit in to the character of our neighborhood.

Oh, my goodness! The way the reporter wrote up the story made my wife sound like an elitist snob. A few days later, they ran a cartoon of our house as a castle and the store as a thatched hut with the caption "There goes the neighborhood." The neoconservative columnist for the paper wrote an editorial accusing my wife of being an economic racist. It was a mess. With no route, that one comment created a huge pile of garbage and pulled the group onto a nasty side trip that nearly killed their message before they even got off the ground.

That's what made me realize how important a route is, whether it's for a volunteer project or a marriage or any other part of my life. I need focus and direction if I don't want my goals and plans to end up in a ditch on the side of the road. It's like that old saying: "If you don't know where you're going, you'll go anywhere." With life being so busy and time being so valuable, do I really want to leave everything to chance, or do I want to control the direction I'm headed in?

THE CURSE OF THE COMFORT ZONE

My goal is to replace the old garbage in my head with new TBOs so I can create a new me. However, I first have to define who that new person is. Here's the problem: The way my brain is wired, it loves its comfort zone and has no interest in altering who I am or how I think.

When I say comfort zone, I mean a warm, safe place that lets my mind say, "I like it here and I'm *not* changing." Comfort zones hate anything that's new. Start asking questions like "Where do I want to take my life?" and your comfort zone will race to the front of your brain, wave its arms like a crazy person, and shout, "Don't listen to that! You're fine right where you are!"

Comfort zones thrive on garbage: outdated TBOs that they can use to scare and intimidate me into keeping things exactly the way they are. So what if a relationship is rocky or an activity is boring? My comfort zone doesn't care. It wants me to think my life is great even though I realize, at some gut level, that I want more.

Here's a story about comfort zones. There was this kid named Thomas. He was really smart and had some great ideas on products and services. When his family fell on hard times and had to move to a new town, Thomas thought of a zillion ways he could earn money to help the family. However, his mom wanted him to stay focused on his studies. Afraid to disappoint her, he stayed in his comfort zone and put the kibosh on his creativity, even though it tore him up inside to do that.

Nothing ventured, nothing gained. High risk, high reward. These old sayings are carrots designed to lure me out of my comfort zone. They are also a warning: Avoid creating a route and stay anchored in my comfort zone, and it will be very hard to reach my dreams.

WHERE CHANGE HAPPENS

We grow up with people telling us what to do. Eat your vegetables. Clean your room. Empty the kitchen garbage. At some point, we have to take over that process and start to tell ourselves what to do. That means making our own decisions about what we want and where we should go to get it.

IF I'M AT A AND I WANT TO GET TO B, I HAVE TO BELIEVE SO STRONGLY IN B THAT I'LL DO WHATEVER IT TAKES TO GET THERE.

If I'm at A and I want to get to B, I have to believe so strongly in B that I'll do whatever it takes to get there. The force inside of me that makes that happen is my belief system. My belief system is the part of my mind that believes with 100 percent certainty that I have already become the person of my goals and dreams, even though I may not actually be there yet.

Let me give you an example. I had a friend named George who wanted to take a trip to the Grand Canyon, which meant a lot of hiking and walking. George wasn't in the best of shape and needed to drop about thirty pounds, so he started a diet. And a second one. And a third one. No matter what he did, the weight wouldn't come off. What finally changed it for him was focusing on *how* he was eating instead of *what* he was eating. His belief system tattooed the phrase "I am a person who eats well" right on his brain, so when he looked at a bag of cookies, he'd say to himself, "If I'm someone who eats well, it would be completely unlike me to wolf down five of them." Once he started thinking like that, the weight began to come off.

> CHANGE HAPPENS WHEN I STOP DOING THINGS BECAUSE PEOPLE TELL ME TO AND INSTEAD, I START DOING THEM BECAUSE I WANT TO.

Change happens when I stop doing things because people tell me to and instead, I start doing them because I want to. When I realize that I'm in the driver's seat and I'm in control of my life, trash stops building up in my head. My Empty Zones no longer bulge with random TBOs because I know I'm responsible for what I let in there. And I choose only those TBOs that take me to the places I want to go in my life.

That's what it means to create a route. It's inventing a brand new me that doesn't exist yet and, at the same time, believing with every cell in my body that I already am that new me. If you create timid, unconstructive TBOs like *Someday, I might become that person* or *I'm not sure I can change that much but I'll try,* you'll undermine any chance you have of actually getting there—and the old garbage will win time and time again.

THE SOLUTION: CREATING A ROUTE

The antidote to comfort zones is a route. For a waste hauling company, creating a route begins by carving up a city into neighborhoods. Then, the company assigns goals: pick up 100 percent of the garbage in West Benson on Monday, Riverdale on Tuesday, and so on. Then they take action, like sending Joe in truck 433 to West Benson to do the work.

I do the same thing when I create a personal route. First, I break my life into segments like Family, Career, or Hobby. Then, I set goals for each of those segments. What do I want to accomplish in my job? Where do I want my marriage to be in three years? Then, I start taking action, throwing out any trash that blocks my way. Once I add this kind of organization to my life, some pretty amazing things start to happen.

For starters, just having a plan puts my mind at ease. I don't have to guess anymore. All the different pieces of my life start working together. I develop a rhythm, getting to know which thoughts and beliefs keep me humming along and which ones get in my way.

Routes are also great confidence builders for me. Because they're goal-driven, I know what I've already accomplished and what I still need to get done. Routes help me hone in on what I truly want, which means I can clearly see the garbage that's in my way of getting it.

ROUTES ARE GREAT CONFIDENCE BUILDERS.

Here's another thing that surprised me. At first, I thought creating personal routes would pigeonhole me. If it's all mapped out, there's no room for spontaneity, right? Actually, I found that the opposite is true. With my head no longer spinning from the *Where am I going?* frenzy, I felt a lot freer to improvise. Instead of this constant feeling that I was missing something, I took all that energy and plowed it back into my goals, where I found I was far more flexible to deal with the unexpected.

I also learned that the goals I set for my routes don't have to be huge or life altering. Sure, I want to push myself. At the same time, I want to get to the finish line! That's not going to happen if I set huge, lofty goals that will take an act of Congress before I can reach them. Big change can come from small steps. Take baseball players. The difference between a .250 and a .350 batting average can be as little as one hit per week over the course of the season. *One hit!*

That's not very much. But the salary difference between a guy hitting .350 versus someone hitting .250? Huge!

EXPANDING THE COMFORT ZONE

Okay. I've created a route by segmenting my life and setting goals. I put my mental truck in gear and start to take action. Pretty soon, this feeling wells up inside of me when I realize that I'm out of my comfort zone—way out! Nothing feels familiar anymore. And let me tell you, that is seriously intimidating when you're not used to it.

Remember when I said earlier that I had to believe that I already was the person I'm trying to become? This is where that really comes into play. It might sound strange—start acting like your future self before you've hit your goals—but if anything is going to prevent me from running back to my comfort zone, it's this. The more I believe that I'm a new person on the inside, the more power I have to dump the negative TBOs that have been driving my old behavior. Here's a great example of how this works.

Meet Charlotte. She's a very talented engineer who wants to become a department manager. So she asked her boss for some extra responsibility and found herself in charge of a large, important meeting. And wouldn't you know it: Everything that could go wrong, did go wrong. The conference call had technical glitches. Two key managers didn't like her ideas and shredded her in front of the entire group. Here she was, taking her first step out of her

| COMFORT ZONE | *Uncomfortable Situation #1* | GOAL |

→

comfort zone, and *wham!* She ran head-on into her first uncomfortable situation.

Stinging from the experience, Charlotte went home that night, flopped onto the couch, and started mulling over what happened. The day's events kept replaying themselves in her head over and over again like a really bad song. This is where choice and Charlotte's belief system come into play. She can look at what happened and be victimized by it, or she can walk away with some valuable new knowledge about herself and what took place.

If Charlotte truly believed that she was a department manager (even though she isn't yet), she would dissect the situation in order to learn everything she could about it. She'd ask why things went sideways, question how she handled the situation, and decide what she could do better. With her belief system repeating *You're a manager* over and over again, she would know that the more she learned from this uncomfortable event, the stronger of a manager she'd become.

Thinking that way increases the size of her comfort zone to include the bad experience. It morphs from a crummy day where she's beating herself up to a great learning experience and a lesson on what not to do next time. *That doesn't mean she's not reacting*

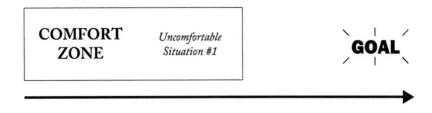

to what happened or experiencing all the feelings of frustration and disappointment. She's human. All those feelings are pounding through her. But they're not in control of her anymore! She feels them—and she moves on. End result: She stays on the route to becoming a department manager.

When Charlotte hits the next uncomfortable situation, she'll put to work all the lessons she just learned. Her comfort zone will expand yet again to include this second experience, putting her even further along the route to her goals. As a bonus, she'll get through the issue faster because there won't be any garbage in her way. All of this is possible because she started believing she was the department manager—even though she hadn't landed the job yet.

What happens if Charlotte doesn't learn much from the botched meeting? Essentially, she's the same person she was before, *wishing* that she was different instead of *becoming* someone different. Her comfort zone doesn't expand. She makes very little progress on her route. The garbage is still in control. When she hits the next uncomfortable situation, she'll probably react the same way and get the same results, so there's no forward progress.

LEARNED	DIDN'T LEARN
Wrestle	Wallow
Fight	Give In
Accept Responsibility	Blame
Talk	Justify
Question	Self-Shred
Different Behavior	**Same Behavior**

Remember Thomas, the smart, creative kid who really wanted to help out his family? When he turned sixteen, he took a night job, not just to earn money, but to start tapping into some of his talent and drive that had been pent up for so long. One night, while exploring an idea for a new product, he spilled some sulfuric acid. It ran between the floorboards and dripped onto his boss's desk below, eating right through it. The next morning, they fired him. But that didn't stop him.

Thomas moved into the basement of a friend's house so he wouldn't be a drain on his family anymore. For a long time, he really struggled. Money was hard to come by. However, he never stopped believing that he was a successful businessman who could create great things. Three years after he left home, Thomas patented his first invention. He started a company to try to sell his new product, and he attracted some pretty big backers to help him. A few years after that, the money was flowing in and he had a reputation as being a focused, bright entrepreneur.

It's human nature to dive back into the comfort zone after a nasty experience. The key is not to get stuck there. If I tell myself to stay on my route no matter what, I can get through anything life throws at me.

ROUTE MANAGEMENT SYSTEM

There's a saying that businesspeople all over the world are taught: If you can't measure it, you can't manage it. In the world of waste hauling, that's known as route management. Using data provided by on-board computers and GPS devices, the office knows where each truck is and exactly what it's doing.

I use the same Route Management System to check in on my own routes and make sure they're moving me in the right direction.

1. **Figure out where I am.**

To plot out a route, I first need to know exactly where I am. I do the same thing that we do at work: carve up my life into segments just like our route manager carves up our city into neighborhoods. A segment is a part of my life that's so important, I want to set goals for it. Some segments are permanent, such as Parent, Spouse, or Career. Other segments are temporary, such as Volunteer.

After I lay out my segments, I ask myself where I am in each one, kind of like taking a picture. What's working and what isn't in my marriage? How do I want to change the way I'm parenting my kids? I'm not worried about the answers I turn up, even if I don't like some of them. All I care about is getting an accurate read of exactly where I am in each of the important areas of my life.

2. Figure out where I want to be.

The next step in creating a route is deciding where I want to be. That's where goals come in. For each segment, I ask myself a simple question: "Where do I want to be in twelve months?" Whatever I choose, I make sure it's a real challenge, or I'm not going to be motivated enough to get off my duff and make something happen. This is a real chance for me to look beyond the low-hanging fruit and reach for the really big things that I want. Setting a low bar isn't going to cut it.

Once I've written out my goals for each of my segments, I stand back and ask, "Do all of these add up to the life I want to live?" Then, I dig deep before answering. I wrestle with what I want. I kick my goals around the block a few times. And I don't stop until I get it right.

3. Engage my belief system.

Remember when we talked about the belief system? Here's where it really kicks into gear.

To cement my commitment to a route, I need an absolute, unshakable belief in the direction I'm headed. I have to start imagining that I am the person that I'm trying to become—segment by segment, regardless of the fact that I'm not there yet. In other words, if I want to be different, I have to believe that I am different.

Once my belief system is truly engaged, my brain starts working like crazy to close the gap between the person I am today and the person I'm trying to become. I start dumping unhelpful TBOs left and right that are trying to yank me off my route onto some unproductive side trip. That's the beauty of being anchored in my belief system: I blow by roadblocks like they're not even there.

4. Physically exit the comfort zone.

I've segmented my life, set some goals, and supported myself with my belief system. Now, it's time to take action—and that means leaving my comfort zone.

That sounds a whole lot easier than it is—especially if my mind is saying, "I ain't budging!" When this happens, I've found that the best thing to do is to get myself out of my normal routine. I'll surprise my wife with a weekend at the beach or try some weird new restaurant—anything to shake up the routine. I'm not trying to move mountains here. All I want to do is push my mind to a different place. Like a truck on a really cold day, it may creak and groan for a little while, but eventually it'll move.

5. Mentally exit the comfort zone.

If I'm going to make my route a reality, I need to "brainwash" my belief system into accepting that I am a changed person. That means mental imagery, which goes by a lot of different names: manifestation, visualization, or affirmations. Whatever you call it, it's designed to do one thing: convince my brain that I'm headed in a new direction and nothing is going to stop me.

An affirmation is a statement that I absolutely, 100 percent believe is true. If my sports segment goal is to finish a 10K race, my affirmation can be as simple as "I am a runner." Have I ever done a 10K? Nope. Have I started my training yet? Doesn't matter. What's important is that I'm telling that stubborn brain of mine in no uncertain terms that *I am a runner.* I do that by visualizing myself on the course, feet beating on the pavement or crossing the finish line. I repeat the affirmation over and over until my brain begins to accept it as a new TBO. I know it's a little like putting the cart before the horse, but trust me on this one. Do this regularly and the horse will always catch up!

Affirmations work because they paint a picture that's way bigger than the person I am right now. That gives my mind a place to aim. It pounds home the *I have changed* message so clearly that my mind automatically throws out any garbage that doesn't fit. It's like a self-fulfilling prophecy. If I convince myself that I've changed, I've changed. If I think I'm a new person, I'm a new person.

SEGMENT	GOAL	AFFIRMATION
Career	Be the department manager within six months.	"Managing people is effortless."
Spouse	Reignite the passion in my marriage.	"I am a very romantic person."
Parenting	Have fewer fights with my teenage son.	"I am a patient listener, no matter what I'm hearing."
Volunteer	Become president of my local library association.	"I am a motivational, seasoned leader."

Then, it's drill sergeant time. I repeat the affirmations—say, three to five times a day for at least three weeks. I don't just let myself read the words or let the image flash through my mind. I want to burn it into my brain, so I close my eyes, take a few deep breaths, and really focus on what I'm telling myself.

Here are some other ways I work affirmations into my day.

- I picked up a bulletin board and hung it on the wall at home. Then, I took the answers to the "What do I want?" questions I asked in Step 2 and pinned them up on the board. Every few days, I look them over to remind myself of the direction I'm headed.

- If I'm feeling bummed out about something—say, I'm beating myself up about being cash-strapped—I'll tape a picture of Disneyland on the bathroom mirror to remind me of the vacation we're saving for. Or I'll write "All the money stuff will work its way out" on a Post-it note and stick it on the dashboard of my truck. A simple, positive message like that really helps steer me back onto my route.

- I'll write down a goal I'm shooting for, take a picture of it, and use it as a background image on my phone or as a screensaver for my computer.

My affirmations can be about what I want or who I want to be, so it doesn't matter what the subject is: improving my credit score, losing some weight, or being a better parent. Because they remind me of what I really want out of life, affirmations keep me motivated and on track—which I really need sometimes.

And let me tell you, this stuff works. My wife's friend pasted pictures of hundred-dollar bills and the number $72,500 on the wall—the amount of money she wanted to make at her job. When her next performance review came up, they told her she had been promoted. Guess what her new salary was? That's right: $72,500. Now, I'm not saying that there's magic happening here or that a piece of paper taped to the mirror will guarantee an outcome. What I've learned though, is that I usually attract what I think about. If I'm negative, that's what usually shows up. If I truly believe I can accomplish something, I almost always do.

> I USUALLY ATTRACT WHAT I THINK ABOUT.

For me, affirmations help my actions line up around my goals. Garbage that used to stop me now gets shoved aside. I know: old dogs, new tricks. But I'm telling you, when I'm dedicated and committed, affirmations are a great way to keep what I want front and center.

USE CAUTION

Here's a list of potential problems that can interfere with my ability to create a route.

Avoid Side Trips

It's so easy to let distractions pull me off my route! Just like a flashing neon sign that grabs my attention at night, it's really hard to stay on course sometimes. Here are four temptations that pull me onto a side trip—and what I usually do to head them off.

Avoidance. Ever had a situation that you really didn't want to deal with? That is prime territory for a side trip. Unfortunately, sticking my head in the sand will not get me to the finish line. When I'm in avoidance mode, I remind myself of times I've weathered storms in my life and always made it through to the other side. I challenge myself to uncover why I'm really ducking the situation. And I remind myself of my goals. That's usually enough to get me back on track again.

Hard work. Emptying garbage is hard work. Cans are heavy. Trucks are bulky. Trash is messy. When it's four o'clock in the morning and I'm rolling out of bed to go to work, it's pretty easy to question whether it's worth the effort.

Personal routes are no walk in the park either. If they are truly challenging, they can be very hard paths to follow. However, there's a dignity to hard work, whether it's emptying cans or emptying TBOs. And I've learned that some of my best results come from some of my toughest challenges. When I feel beat down from all the hard work I'm doing, I remind myself of the contribution I'm making to my family, to the community, and to myself.

Monotony. Sometimes, the monotony of my daily life takes all the air out of my routes. When that happens, it's so easy to chase the flashy allure of something more interesting. Once I notice that I'm bored, I give into it. I let my mind wander. I work out a problem. I think up new goals. Sometimes, I've gotten some pretty great ideas when I'm bored silly.

Emotion. Emotions can take me on major side trips. Something happens that pops my cork, and suddenly I'm acting way out of character and people around me are running for the hills.

I know I'm not the only one who does this. Remember Thomas? One of his inventions had some pretty serious market potential. Folks were interested in what he was doing but it hadn't caught on yet. He had one competitor: an equally aggressive entrepreneur whose product did the exact same thing, but in a different way. To make things worse, the competitor had licensed patents from one of Thomas's former employees. Instead of sticking to his sales and marketing game plan, Thomas let it get to him personally.

What kinds of side trips do you allow yourself to go on?

He started a nasty public campaign that dissed his rival and the other invention. Thomas let his emotion take him on a side trip that eventually cost him a lot of money when his rival's invention became the industry standard.

Emotional side trips are usually reactions to someone or something. When I find myself in the middle of one, I use the Empty and Return Action Plan from Step 2 to help me break free. I've got too much that I want to accomplish in the short time I'm here. Emotional side trips just don't fit into the plan.

WATCH OUT FOR BLIND SPOTS

My truck has blind spots: places where it's really tough to see other vehicles on the road. Sure, I want to finish my route, but I want to do it safely—for me and for everyone else.

I can say the same thing about my life. I have blind spots everywhere:

- I have habits or ways I act that I don't even notice.

- I look at a situation and see what I want to see, blinding myself to what's really there.

- I keep making the same mistake over and over again, yet I can't see why.

- I try to convince myself that a person, situation, or activity is just fine even though I know it's really not.

- I latch on to an expectation or a desire that doesn't have a prayer of working out.

Here's how I fight blind spots. First, I never forget that I have them. By reminding myself that they exist, I'm minimizing the chances that they can get me into hot water. Second, I use my mirrors to help me see. In my personal life, that can be talking with friends or reading books like this one—anything that can shine a light on the way I'm acting so I can see it and improve it.

Don't Dismiss

Affirmations. Comfort zones. Visualizations. When I first heard about all of this, I shook my head and said to myself, "Um…that's a little out there." That was when a friend of mine gave me some great down-to-earth advice: Don't dismiss it until you've tried it.

After digging a little, I found out that visualizing is rooted in ancient civilizations. Paying attention to my mental chatter is the foundation of several major philosophies. Accepting responsibility for one's own life is the cornerstone of the modern personal growth movement. Millions of people use these techniques every day, so I figured it was probably worth a try.

DON'T DISMISS IT UNTIL YOU'VE TRIED IT.

And you know what? Sticking my toe in unfamiliar waters makes me less likely to reject other new things I come across. There's no harm in that, especially if it helps me toss my mental trash.

As we wrap up this chapter, I have a confession to make. The "Thomas" in my story is actually Thomas Edison, the brilliant inventor. From his humble beginnings selling candy and newspapers on trains, Edison went on to invent the phonograph, a commercial-grade light bulb, new telegraphs, and a way to bring electricity into homes and businesses. He formed dozens of companies, including General Electric, which is still one of the largest publicly traded companies in the world.

Edison had a ton of failures along his route. But that never stopped him because he always believed in a bigger vision of himself and what he could accomplish. "If I find 10,000 ways something won't work, I haven't failed," he once said. "I am not discouraged, because every wrong attempt discarded is another step forward." Edison is a great example of what happens when I create a vision for myself and live it as if it's already come true.

The Last Word

We've just finished covering the first three steps of dumping mental trash:

1. Find the Value and Toss That Trash. I take a thought, belief, or opinion and decide if it has any value to me. If there is none, I toss it.

2. Keep It Empty. Once I toss garbage into my landfill, I create emptiness in my head that I want to leave open for a while.

3. Create Your Route. I set a course for the different parts of my life. If a TBO shows up to fill my emptiness and it doesn't line up with that course, I toss it.

These three steps form the core of tossing my trash and getting out of the dumps. I draw on my Inner Garbageman to keep these three steps in motion.

The rest of the steps in this book are like signs along the road, giving me specific information about how to manage my trash flow and what warning signs I should look out for. If I stand back and look at the eight steps together, some important themes start to appear.

First, I need to become acutely aware of the thoughts, beliefs, and opinions running through my mind. What I think expands into my life. It defines who I am and how the world sees me, and it creates the reality that I live in every day. If a lion's share of my thoughts are based on negative, self-defeating TBOs, it's going to be really hard to reach my goals. It's like driving with one foot on the gas and the other one on the brake. I'm going to chew up a lot of energy and still not get anywhere. If I want to create something different for myself, I have to pay attention to what's going on in my head. That's what my Inner Garbageman is for. He helps me see the trash and he gets rid of it.

Second, I need to remember that nearly all of my TBOs were formed around events from my past. They're like a forty-year-old garbage truck, still in use way past the time when it should have been retired and taken off the road. To me, the past is nothing more than a collection of old memories and feelings about events that took place a long time ago. It's not real. It's not tangible. I can't reach out and touch it. Plus, my mind isn't a computer that can pull up the event and replay it exactly like it happened. Memory fades over time and emotion changes my recollection of what happened. So the way I remember my past may be very different from what actually took place.

Finally, managing my inner garbage boils down to some simple choices. What do I want to carry around every day? What do I want to leave behind? What's weighing me down? The TBOs I keep in my head ultimately determine the amount of garbage that's going to haunt me. Whether I keep or toss that trash is my choice and my responsibility. Books like this one can explain the process, and my team can help me along the way, but at the end of the day, it's my life and it's up to me to shape it.

TAKING IT TO THE STREET

SUMMARY: CREATE YOUR ROUTE

As I tap into my Inner Garbageman, my goal is to toss the trash I don't need anymore and fill the Empty Zones I've created with new TBOs that support what I really want out of life. At the same time, these TBOs need to have a context—a place I can point to and say, *"That's* who I want to be." If I'm not clear about where I'm going, I'll end up with a jumble of positive thoughts that don't hang together. I may feel better about myself, but I'll have no idea where I might end up.

That's where a route comes in. It forces me to sit down and map out where I am and where I want to go. Once I get there, I know I'll be a different person because I will have taken on new responsibilities and expanded my horizons.

A route pulls me out of my comfort zone. Because I now know what I want, it becomes much easier to see the garbage that's blocking me from getting it. Routes give me something to shoot for. They build my confidence and strengthen my ability to weather any storm that life throws my way.

> BECAUSE I NOW KNOW WHAT I WANT, IT BECOMES MUCH EASIER TO SEE THE GARBAGE THAT'S BLOCKING ME FROM GETTING IT.

Routes also come with a few house rules in order to be truly effective. I have to be totally committed to my goals or they become mere wishes with a small likelihood of ever coming true. Once I set a goal, I have to act like I've already completed it, even though that hasn't happened yet. The more I believe, the more I'll reprogram myself on a subconscious level that I'm a changed person. That's when I start thinking and acting differently, which ultimately rockets me toward completing my goals.

To create and monitor the progress of my route, I break my life into segments like Marriage and Career, figure out where I am in each of those segments, and then decide where I want to be by setting goals for each one. Next, I plug in my belief system and start taking action. To prevent my comfort zone from holding me back, I train my body and my mind to push their boundaries. This toughens me up for the inevitable roadblocks and potholes that I'm going to hit along the way.

As I travel along my new route, I need to watch out for side trips that will pull me off course. Most important, I stick to my route no matter how bumpy the road may get.

EXERCISES

1. **Make a list of the segments that represent each of the major areas of your life.**

_____

_____

_____

_____

_____

_____

_____

_____

2. **For each segment, write down at least one goal that you want to accomplish within the next six months.**

_____

_____

_____

_____

_____

3. **For each segment, write down at least one thing you could do to push yourself out of your comfort zone.**

_____

_____

_____

_____

_____

4. **For each goal, write down at least one affirmation. Then, create a way you'll remind yourself of that affirmation every day.**

_____

_____

_____

_____

_____

5. List the kinds of side trips you take most often and what you can do to stop them.

    _____

    _____

    _____

    _____

    _____

6. Make a list of the blind spots you think you have. (I highly recommend checking in with a few trusted friends or colleagues to help you with this exercise.)

    _____

    _____

    _____

    _____

    _____

STEP 4
PARK YOUR EGO

---

*"The ego relies on the familiar. It is reluctant to experience the
unknown, which is the very essence of life."*
—Deepak Chopra

A few years back, about two hours into my Tuesday route, I got
a call on the radio from one of our customer service agents. She told
me that I had missed a can on Ridgewood Street. I thought that was
a little strange because I'm pretty careful about that kind of thing.
But what the heck. Everyone makes mistakes, right? So I turned my
truck around and drove back to the address she gave me, but when
I got there—no can.

A few hours later, my radio went off again. This time, it was the
route supervisor. He told me the guy called in again, miffed that I
still hadn't picked up his can. I could feel myself getting a little hot
under the collar. I told him that I had driven back to the guy's house
and I couldn't find a can. We went back and forth a few more times,
and that was that.

Well, guess what? I was almost done with my route when my
boss radioed me. "Listen," he said in a very annoyed voice, "this

guy has called us three times in a row and said you keep missing his can!"

I couldn't believe this! I had been picking up trash for years. Why didn't they believe me? I mean, this whole thing had been blaring across the company radio all day long, for everyone to hear. By this point, I didn't know who was crazier: the homeowner with the mystery can or the folks back in the office who kept hassling me about this. And to make matters worse, I was clear across town by this point.

"It doesn't matter," my boss told me. "Go get the can!" To say that I was annoyed was an understatement. I hung up the microphone and fought my way through traffic until I got to this guy's house. Sure enough, no can. I hopped out of the truck just as he came out the front door. "There's nothing here!" I said to him, trying very hard to be polite. "Why do you keep phoning the office and telling them that I'm not doing my job?"

"What are you talking about?" the man said. "My can is right over there!" The moment he walked me over to it, I wasn't sure whether to be amused or embarrassed.

This guy lived on a corner lot. Instead of putting his can on Ridgewood Street, he rolled it around to the other side and left it sitting on Miller Road. And we don't pick up Miller on Tuesday.

Man, what a lesson *that* was. I was so focused on Ridgewood that I never even turned to look the other way. And no one in the office tried to figure out what happened, either. They just expected me to fix it. Here we are, paid to solve problems for our customers, and what did we do? Defended ourselves and our opinions, no matter what. One glance down the street or one peek at a map and we could have nailed this problem instead of chewing up radio time and burning diesel.

You know who that is, the guy who plants his flag and defends his turf? That's my ego. I can throw trash into my landfill, generate emptiness, and create as many routes as I want. But if my ego is in the driver's seat, I'm not going anywhere. That's why learning to park my ego has been one of the most valuable lessons I've learned from being a garbageman. And that's what I want to pass on to you. Once I figured out how my ego worked, it became so much easier for me to manage it. That helped me keep my garbage under control—and it can do exactly the same thing for you.

THE PERFECT GARBAGEMAN

A while back, the management team challenged all the drivers in our company to find ways to improve our level of service, so we got together and started kicking around ideas. A while into it, someone piped up and said that he felt like management was trying to create the perfect garbageman. We all grumbled with him for a while. Most of us have been on the job for a long time, busting hump eight hours a day, sometimes six days a week. Why was that not good enough anymore?

Then, I started thinking about what makes a perfect garbageman. He gets to work on time. He has a great safety record. He hardly ever misses a pickup. Inside the company, he doesn't get on people's nerves, and he doesn't get defensive when someone hands him some good, solid suggestions on how he can run a better route. That sounded a lot like the Inner Garbageman I talked about earlier in the book. Suddenly, it hit me. We could be ticked off by this exercise—just another attempt by management to squeeze more work out of us—or we could take it on as a challenge to improve the way we serve our customers and our company.

My brain does this all the time, bouncing back and forth between openness and being dug in. It's like my ego is always doing battle with my Inner Garbageman. The more I looked, the more I realized that this tug-of-war has been going on my whole life. And it's a major obstacle to emptying my mental trash and staying out of the dumps. So I started comparing my Inner Garbageman to my ego, and I discovered some very interesting things that I want to share with you.

LET'S TALK EGO

For starters, the ego is very me-centric, plopping me in the middle of everything and driven solely on what I want and what I need. My ego loves to run the show. Give it a microphone and a spotlight and it will hog the stage for as long as it can.

Ego is a creature of habit. It's an autopilot that wants me to react the same way all the time because it hates change. It's spent years collecting TBOs and putting its own spin on them, so the last thing it wants is for me to start rearranging my mental furniture.

Ego is both smart and stubborn. It knows that the more I hang out with my Inner Garbageman, the closer I'll come to ending its hypnotic grip on the way I think and act. That means my ego will do anything it can to resist dumping trash and creating Empty Zones. When I hear myself saying, "I'm too tired" or "I don't want to deal with this right now," I know that's my ego trying to yank me off track. Ego doesn't care about my soul or my long-term goals or staying on my route. It only cares about getting by.

What automatic behaviors do you have? What limits do you think they have placed on you?

My ego constantly needs stroking. Sometimes, when I finish an ordinary project like cleaning up the yard, I want to grab the first person who walks by and make him admire my work. I mean, it would be a catastrophe if no one paid attention to me, right? That's my ego in all its glory. It thinks "unnoticed" means "unimportant," and it can't take that. Never mind that my job is absolute proof that unnoticed can be incredibly important. (Imagine what life would be like if all the garbage companies stopped picking up the trash.) Unfortunately, that kind of logic is totally wasted on my ego because it's not programmed to look for satisfaction from within me. It needs the world out there to tell it that I matter and that I'm important.

Here's another thing about ego. It does not want the world to see my Inner Garbageman at all. It's embarrassed by how honest and straightforward it is. It's afraid that I'll be judged or rejected if I'm that open with everyone. Plus, my ego thinks that putting my real self out there is way too scary—and it's suspicious of anything that drags it out of its comfort zone.

EARLY ORIGINS

My ego started to form when I was a kid and I felt defenseless. It was like having my own knight who was always by my side, sword drawn, ready to defend me. *Thwack!* Cover up fear of failure. *Clang!* Hide away fear of not fitting in. My ego taught me how to put on a brave face so the world didn't think I was afraid. That gave me a thick skin and the street smarts to make it through some pretty tough times growing up.

Here's the problem. Ego was meant to be short-term protective armor. It was never meant to be worn permanently. At some point, my brain was supposed to say, "Oh. This behavior is my ego trying to protect me, but I don't need its help in this particular situation." However, no one ever taught me to think like that. So there I was, letting my ego fill my inexperienced little mind with TBOs without ever realizing that I was supposed to let them go at some point.

Years pass by and my ego is still there, watching out for me. That's a good thing, because in certain circumstances I really need that protection. The problem is that my ego will use whatever weapons it can find—including reaching back and grabbing outdated TBOs that I haven't had a chance to throw into my landfill yet. That's when I start acting and reacting like that defenseless little kid again. It's not that I'm purposely trying to be annoying or immature. It's more like my mind and my feelings are on autopilot, pulling on old, reliable TBOs they're comfortable with. However, if I throw those obsolete TBOs out and create Empty Zones filled with new ways of thinking, my ego won't have access to the old stuff anymore and I can park it. That's when new behavior kicks in and I begin to see different results.

Look back at your childhood. Can you find the origins of some of your adult behavior?

THE MASKS OF EGO

You know what a mask is, right? It's something you wear that hides who you really are. Well, let me tell you something. My ego loves masks. It has a whole collection of them hanging in perfect rows on my mental wall. There's a mask for envy, a mask for anger, and a mask for people pleasing. I have a mask for arrogance (showing up late because I think my time is more valuable than others'), a mask for self-criticism ("You drive a garbage truck. You're not smart enough to help your daughter with her homework"), and a mask for martyrdom (killing my dreams so I live up to other people's expectations).

As situations come at me, my ego starts swapping masks left and right as it reacts to what's going on. My kid is yelling. Parent mask! My wife is upset. Husband mask! Sometimes, it feels like I'm a different person, minute by minute. Don't get me wrong. I'm not knocking my ego. It always gets me through the crisis. However, there's a price I pay when I leave my masks on for too long: hurt feelings, unmet expectations, and strained relationships. I'm so focused on not getting hurt or trying to please everyone else that I never get a chance to take all the masks off and just be myself. To me, that's the biggest cost of all.

When I'm wearing a mask, my perspective is inside out. My ego is peering out at the big, scary world, using the mask like a barrier because it thinks it needs one to cope. That makes sense because the TBOs that I've carried my whole life have trained my ego to believe that masks are the only way to deal with creepy situations. My ego reaches for one automatically, without thinking, just like a mechanic reaches for a wrench.

MY MIND USES MASKS LIKE A BARRIER BECAUSE IT THINKS IT NEEDS ONE TO COPE.

While I'm looking at the world from the inside out, the world is looking at me from the outside in. They don't know what's going on in that crazy brain of mine. All they see is inconsistency. I'm bouncing around from one persona to the next, so people don't quite know what to expect from me. And here's the ironic part. While I think I'm safely hiding behind my mask, they can totally see through it. So the twelve-inch-thick walls I think I'm surrounding myself with are actually nothing more than see-through sheets of plastic wrap.

THE DANGERS OF AN UNCHECKED EGO

Letting my ego run around unchecked has some pretty nasty downsides. For starters, when my ego has me reacting from one situation to the next, it wears me out after a while. I feel like I'm slogging through mud, barely making progress as I drag myself from one situation to the next. Nothing comes easily, and I sure don't feel like I'm at the top of my game.

There's also a ton of anxiety and stress. When my ego is in charge, I'm coping instead of creating, which means I can't predict the kind of results I'm going to get. Not that I have a crystal ball or anything, but I'm far less confident in how things are going to turn out if my ego is throwing its weight around.

Then there's the chaos factor. When I'm running around with my hair on fire, there's one thing I can count on: accidents. I don't want to listen or compromise or admit that the other person might be right. When I dig in like that, there's a very high likelihood that I'm going to do some damage to myself and to the relationships around me.

You know what I dislike the most about my ego? It's a never-ending critic that dwells on everything I do wrong. When I'm in the middle of a situation where I really need some confidence, what does my ego do? Replay all of my embarrassing moments and remind me of all the mistakes I've made. What purpose does that serve? How is a voice in my head that's dredging up all my faults and shortcomings supposed to help me reach my goals? It can't—but I keep listening to it, anyway!

> MY EGO IS A NEVER-ENDING CRITIC THAT DWELLS ON EVERYTHING I DO WRONG.

I will never forget the story my grandfather told me about the time he was in Marine Corps basic training. During one exercise, he was made the temporary platoon leader, in charge of everything. He got the whole platoon ready for inspection and was horrified when the drill sergeant found an apple under someone's pillow. He went ballistic and tore the place apart, humiliating my grandfather in the process.

The next inspection was scheduled for later that day. Just as the platoon was getting ready, the mail arrived. All of a sudden, everyone stopped what they were doing and started reading their letters, which really ticked off my grandfather. All he cared about was not getting in trouble again, so he ran around the barracks, snatching the mail from everyone's hands. It took about ten seconds before he became the most hated person in the room. He said he had no idea how much he'd lost control of himself until one guy whom he really admired looked at him after he grabbed his letter and said, "You know, you're the worst leader I've ever seen."

My grandpa's ego was so afraid of failing again that his behavior totally changed. And he nearly drove himself over the cliff in the process.

THE INNER GARBAGEMAN

Now that we've spent some time exploring ego, let's do the same for the Inner Garbageman. Who is this guy and what does he do for me?

When someone says that I have a good soul or a big heart, I take that to mean that they've seen my Inner Garbageman. It's the real me that's not trying to impress anyone or live up to people's expectations. My Inner Garbageman responds to situations quietly and calmly. He makes conscious choices about what behavior is best for the situation in front of me, which is very different from my ego's "react first and clean up the mess later" way of thinking.

My Inner Garbageman is very confident—not in an arrogant way, but solid in the knowledge of who I am and what I stand for. He keeps humility in front, using ego only when it's needed. For example, if I have to discipline my kids, I might wear my tough love mask for a short period of time. However, my Inner Garbageman never forgets who I really am behind that mask, unlike my ego, which gets lost in the role and turns discipline into a power trip. Center stage isn't important to my Inner Garbageman. It's everything to my ego.

My Inner Garbageman is the part of me that dreams, that sets up a long-term vision for where I want my life to go. He does his best to make sure my actions match my goals. And if those goals aren't working out, my Inner Garbageman admits it honestly, accepts it gracefully, and moves on to create new goals. My ego, on the other hand, relies on old TBOs and emotion to push me in one direction or another without any rhyme or reason. And if I fail, my ego beats me up, blames everyone else, and pouts because it didn't get what it wanted.

Because my Inner Garbageman makes sure I'm well cared for and garbage-free, he's got room to focus on other people around me, whereas my ego tends to be very me-centered. My Inner Garbageman looks inside of me for strength, guidance, and con-

> MY INNER GARBAGEMAN LOOKS INSIDE OF ME FOR STRENGTH, GUIDANCE, AND CONFIDENCE.

fidence. My ego, on the other hand, needs strokes and reassurances from the outside to tell it that it's okay. Ego is surrounded by drama, chaos, and trash. My Inner Garbageman recognizes that trash is an unnecessary burden and it tosses it into my landfill, leaving behind a beautiful, calm emptiness.

My Inner Garbageman is constantly tuned in to the stream of thoughts, beliefs, and opinions running through my head. When he sees me digging around in my old garbage and running off on some crazy side trip, he's the voice in my head that says, "Hey! This TBO you're obsessing about does *not* fit into any of your goals, so why are you wasting your time with it?" Because he's actively monitoring what I'm thinking, my Inner Garbageman keeps me accountable. And I love that.

Sometimes, people ask me if I'm sensitive about the fact that I drive a garbage truck for a living. If my ego were in charge, I would be. However, my Inner Garbageman doesn't care about my job title, the car I drive, or the number of safety awards I've won. He knows that it's not about what I do; it's about *who I am*: my core values, my integrity, and my attitude. I'm a garbageman because it's a good job, it pays well, and it puts food on the table for my family. That's all my Inner Garbageman is concerned about and that's why he's so powerful: He won't let me waste time on anything that undercuts me.

Now, I don't listen to my Inner Garbageman nearly as much as I should. My ego slips into the driver's seat and takes over—and I don't even realize that it's happened.

I CAN ALWAYS COUNT ON MY INNER GARBAGEMAN TO TELL ME THE TRUTH.

Even so, I can always count on my Inner Garbageman to tell me the truth. And that's what rescues me. If I say a goal is important, my Inner Garbageman reminds me of it every time I get off course. He makes sure I'm consistent and focused, and that I give 100 percent, even when I don't want to. Doubts and excuses? Not part of the Inner Garbageman's vocabulary. He just shows up and plays all-out.

Here's a good example of how the ego can grab the wheel from the Inner Garbageman. My wife and I have this good friend named Mary. She had worked at a children's toy company for nearly three years. She said people kept telling her that she was an incredibly valuable part of the team, a star performer who got along with everyone. That didn't surprise me. Mary had one of the strongest work ethics of anyone I've ever met, and she was a genuinely nice woman everyone loved. If there was a person who exuded the best qualities of the Inner Garbageman, it was Mary.

The problem, she told us, was that she never felt like she fit in. When we asked her why, she told us that all the other company executives had known each other since high school and that they were a pretty tight-knit bunch. I asked if they had done anything to keep her on the fringes. She said no; it was just a feeling that she couldn't get rid of. The more we talked, the more I realized it was her ego that was keeping her apart. Once she put on the *I don't fit in* mask, her ego made sure nothing else got through. The company could shower her with one compliment after another, but their words fell on deaf ears.

I know that sounds weird. I usually think of ego in a boasting, "I'm so great" sort of way, but ego can make us feel small and insignificant, too. And in this case, it had full control of Mary and wasn't about to let go.

EGO, INNER GARBAGEMAN, AND PERCEPTION

Let's say I'm in charge of a team project that's going to make major changes to our routes. It has to be finished by the end of the week—and we're behind schedule. To get back on track, I need to get tough with everyone, so I tell them, "Either we get this done or we're all in hot water. Now, what do we have to do to bring this project to the finish line?" When the meeting is over and everyone is walking out of the conference room, they're going to be thinking one of two things about me:

"He's a good guy. He's tough when he needs to be, but I respect him."

Or:

"What a first-class jerk. He's always complaining about how things are never done right. I can't stand working with him."

Same meeting. Two radically different perceptions of me.

In the "good guy" scenario, my Inner Garbageman is driving my behavior. I want to be tough enough to motivate people, but not hammer them into submission. Everyone knows that finishing the project on time is about the team looking good, not about stroking my ego. So when I play the "get tough" card, they know I'm serious. But they also know that I've got their back and that being hard isn't about power or control. I just want the whole team to win. That's why they'll gladly go the extra mile to finish the project because it's one for all and all for one.

The other scenario is pure ego. All people see is yet another outburst and overreaction. I could ask them to name the days of the week and they'll hear it as nothing more than a driver on a power trip, barking orders and trying to impress management. Sure, they might put in the extra effort, but they're doing it in spite of me, not for me.

Because ego and my Inner Garbageman are opposite sides of my personality, it makes sense that they'll create opposite impressions. Sometimes, that impression affects the people around me. Other times, the struggle between ego and my Inner Garbageman leaves its impression on me alone. That can set up some pretty tough internal conflicts, especially when a big issue is involved.

Let's get back to Mary, who still couldn't shake the *I don't belong* feelings that she had. One day, she got an email from a recruiting company in the Midwest that was looking for a top-level manager. She said she stared at the computer screen for a long time, debating with herself whether or not she should apply.

Every time she thought of something positive about the opportunity—a promotion, more money, the chance to move to a new city—her ego would fire off a counter-volley like, "Why would a big company be interested in *you?*" She said her brain was flooded with old memories: the time she was trounced when she ran for student body president or the pile of college rejection letters that said, "No. You can't come here." She said her finger hovered over the Delete key as her ego fought her Inner Garbageman, debating whether or not to answer the email or trash it.

A BIG SHIFT IN GEARS

There are a lot of good reasons for me to park my ego, but one rises above them all: humility.

A while ago, I was doing my first 15K long-distance run. Even though I had trained like crazy for it, the run was way harder than I had expected. We were two-thirds through the race and I was in agony. Everything hurt and I was hobbling like an old man. The voice in my head just wouldn't quit. "You suck at this. You should never have signed up for a race this long."

Pretty soon, I heard voices behind me. It was a couple, chatting away like there was no tomorrow. It didn't take long before I got annoyed. Everyone around me was being quiet and respectful, trying to get through the last leg of the run, and here's this chatty, happy-go-lucky pair breaking everyone's concentration.

As they moved closer to me, I started to hear what the woman was saying: "Pothole to your left. Go straight. Person crossing in front of you." I turned and looked at her. Despite her chipper voice, she was soaked with sweat and she looked worse than I did. Then, I looked at her running partner.

He was blind.

I realized that this woman had spent every minute of those 9.3 miles calling out directions to her friend so he wouldn't hurt himself. And despite my aches and pains, that remarkable man had run the entire race in complete darkness.

I can't find a better way to show you the contrast between the Inner Garbageman and the ego. There I was, feeling sorry for myself while my ego hammered away at me. I had no energy, no desire, and no passion. It took a blind man and selfless woman for me to see what life looks like when the Inner Garbageman is in control.

That's the great lesson in all of this. It's never too late to get to know my Inner Garbageman. It doesn't matter how old I am or where I am in life. What's important is that I can lean on my Inner Garbageman to pull me out of the dumps and keep me on my route. Listen, I'm a stubborn mule. I want to choose my own course, not have my ego push me into a direction I don't want to go. And I'm telling you, when I boot my ego out of the front seat and let my Inner Garbageman drive, I feel like I can take on the whole world.

> IT'S NEVER TOO LATE TO GET TO KNOW MY INNER GARBAGEMAN.

Here's a chart that summarizes the Inner Garbageman and the ego.

INNER GARBAGEMAN	EGO
Soul and heart	Mind
Calm, quiet, and appropriate responses that I choose	Drama, chaos, and strong autopilot reactions
Humility in front, choosing to use ego as a tool only when it's needed	Ego in front—and wants to stay there; wants to hide the Inner Garbageman
Draws on TBOs aligned with goals	Relies on old TBOs and emotion
Creates a balance between other people and me	Me-centered
Looks within	Looks outward
Very little garbage	Lots of garbage

Let's go back to Mary's story. She responded to the recruiter's email and said she'd like to interview for the job. She told us the process was like a dream: a first-class ticket to the company's headquarters, being treated like a rock star, and everyone excited about her background. It continued when she got the offer letter: a great salary, awesome benefits, and this line: "We look forward to the unique contributions an executive of your caliber will bring to our team." Talk about an ego booster!

So she packed her bags and moved to the Midwest. She'd been on the job for just two days when she was invited to a strategy meeting led by the CEO. He asked her what she thought about the company's sales and marketing plan. Well, she jumped right in and went after everything: pricing, the sales force, all the marketing materials. She even criticized a company ad she had seen in a magazine on the plane ride over. After all, that offer letter had set some pretty high expectations and she wanted to make sure she lived up to them.

Mary told us that after the meeting, the vice president of sales and marketing asked to speak to her. He was furious. He tore into her, accusing her of popping off about things she didn't know about—especially since she hadn't had a single meeting with him or any of his hard-working staff. She said she'd never forget the vice president's last line before he threw her out of his office: "Maybe everyone in your old company did things on their own. Around here, we work as a team, which means we check our egos at the door."

THE PARKSAFE ACTION PLAN

I'll be the first one to put up my hand and tell you that parking my ego is not easy. Once it's hogged the stage, it's hard to shut it down. That's why I created the ParkSafe Action Plan. Its four steps help me wrestle control away from my ego, park it, and safely hand over the keys to my Inner Garbageman. The more I do that, the more balance I have. And believe me, in the long run, that's a lot better for my sanity!

1. Do an audit.

When our crew needs to make route improvements, the first thing we do is an audit. How long are all the pickups taking? Where is traffic slowing us down? What mistakes and problems keep cropping up? We only make changes to the routes after we've asked the questions and analyzed the answers.

The ParkSafe Action Plan works the same way. To find out whether my Inner Garbageman or my ego is in control, I start with an internal audit.

- What key events in my life shaped my core TBOs? How much control do they have over the way I think?

- What am I doing more: reacting or responding?

- How would people describe me: even-keeled and consistent, or emotional and unpredictable?

- Where do I look for confidence: inside myself or through other people?

- What are the masks I wear all the time? What makes me put them on? How easily do I take them off once the situation has passed?

When I do this kind of an audit, I'm brutally honest. Otherwise, I'm just kidding myself about who's really behind the wheel: my ego or my Inner Garbageman. And if I find myself cutting corners and dancing around the truth, I pretty much have my answer.

You know the safety demonstration they do on an airplane before it takes off? They always tell you to put your oxygen mask on first before helping someone else. That's exactly what the audit is all about. It puts the responsibility on me to figure out why I'm acting like I do, to get my own ego in check before I run around and start dealing with everyone else.

2. Stop talking and start listening.

Every once in a while, I get into a fight with my wife. (We've been married for twenty years. We're not going to agree on everything!) I've noticed something very interesting about the way those arguments go.

If I'm bullheaded and righteous, it doesn't matter what my wife says to me. Come hell or high water, I'm going to prove to her that this is all her fault. But if I can shut myself up long enough to really listen to what she's saying, guess what? It's never all her. Usually, we both did something that helped create the mess we're in.

That's why one of the fastest ways to park my ego is to stop talking and start listening. The moment I interrupt my own thoughts, I usually find a way to diffuse the situation I'm in and get on with life. The most effective way to do this is to pay attention to my Inner Garbageman, which will be whispering in my head, "Excuse me. You're out of control." I need to turn up the volume on that voice and listen to it rather than ignore it. It's there for a reason.

> ONE OF THE FASTEST WAYS TO PARK MY EGO IS TO STOP TALKING AND START LISTENING.

You know what else helps me? A little reading or web surfing about the human psyche and how it resists change. The more I know about the way my brain works, the easier it is to figure out how to work around the crazy stuff it does. (Don't forget to check out GG-Resources.com. That's a great place to start!) Remember: The goal is to toss my mental trash and create some Empty Zones to clear my mind. Listening is a terrific way to help me do that.

3. Build a team.

Ego wants to go it alone. When I hear, "I don't want to be a burden" or "I can handle it" coming out of my mouth, that's my ego wanting to fly solo again. Here's the truth. Sometimes I'm so tangled up in my own weeds there's no way I can get myself out. That's why I have a few people around me who have total permission to tell me to park my ego. If I'm acting like a jerk, they call me on it. My ego doesn't like it, but I don't care. I want to get to the finish line, and that's not going to happen if my ego has the wheel. Besides, if my friends won't tell me that I'm out of control, who will?

My team changes depending on where I am and what I need. Sometimes it's family or a professional counselor or someone I trust at work. The only thing I ask of them is to be totally honest. I know my ego loves to be soft-shoed and told that life is perfect. This is not the group of people to do that.

4. Practice humility.

Nothing parks my ego faster than a good dose of humility. That's why it's part of the ParkSafe Action Plan.

If someone's trying to merge into my lane, I let them in. If it's five in the morning, I try not to bang the cans around. It doesn't do me any good to rant and rave and draw attention to myself. My job is to serve the public, not tick folks off.

I do my best to bring that modesty into my personal life. If I'm hammering on myself or someone else, I need to back off. If I'm flying off the handle, I need to stop. It's about stepping up and controlling my ego instead of it controlling me. At the end of the day, I'm totally responsible for everything that happens in my life. The last thing I need is an ego running through the glass shop, breaking everything in sight.

For me, it comes down to a simple question: Would I rather be right, or would I rather be happy?

So what happened to Mary after her ego-slaying experience with the vice president? At first, she was horrified by her mistake. She even thought about quitting because she was so embarrassed. But that's not Mary. She's about as tough and humble as they come. After thinking about things, she realized that she'd let the interview and the offer letter go to her head. And she knew she had some cleanup work to do.

First, after she cleared her head, she went straight to the vice president and offered him a sincere apology. Then, for the next few weeks, she did what she does best: listen and learn. She told us that when she felt ready, she went back to the vice president and offered a new set of critiques—not on a bended knee, but with a genuine desire to help the company and to build relationships. She said it was like magic. The vice president loved her ideas, and over time the two of them became quite the duo, rocketing past all the sales numbers. And here's the great part. When it was all said and done,

Mary said that for the first time in ages, she felt like she was part of a team.

USE CAUTION

This is a list of the most common speed bumps I run into when I'm trying to park my ego.

DON'T UNDERESTIMATE YOUR EGO

My ego can be one tough customer. Tell it that I'm going to perform a little mental housecleaning and it will do anything it can to prevent that from happening. That's why I can never underestimate my ego or the flood of old garbage TBOs that it will unleash to try to convince me that everything is fine just the way it is.

At the same time, I don't want to underestimate the ability of my Inner Garbageman to shut that behavior down. I may lose the battle to my ego now and then, but I'm no weakling. As strong as my ego may be, I can own up to my behavior and take back control. So bring on the garbage. I'm ready to throw it out if I need to!

> THE LONGER MY EGO CALLS THE SHOTS, THE WORSE THE SITUATION IS GOING TO GET.

IT IS WHAT IT IS

Sometimes, life stinks. Plans don't work out. Relationships go sideways. Projects crash and burn. When I hit the skids like that, I have no idea how I'm going to make it back to the road.

That's where I need to be careful. When my ego gets in the middle of a mess, it's going to try to spin events to its advantage. It's going to blame everyone else, get defensive, and attempt damage control instead of cleanup. The longer my ego calls the shots, the worse the situation is going to get.

You know what helps? Admitting that I sometimes screw things up, I don't always get it right, and every once in a while I turn left when I should have turned right. Just putting that out there gives me a little breathing room. I'm not making excuses for my behavior or my actions. It's more like I'm accepting the situation at face value. From there, I do what's necessary to clean it up without adding any more garbage to the situation.

Manage Your Self-Talk

I'm amazed when I stop and really listen to the chatter that's running through my head. So much of it is based on fear—thoughts like, "Watch out or something bad will happen!" That's my ego playing "not to lose" and preventing me from taking action.

I know my Inner Garbageman uses an entirely different language, one based on the belief that *I can do this*. But if I don't manage all that self-talk, the power I give my ego drowns out the Inner Garbageman's voice. When I hear familiar excuses or I start rationalizing what I'm doing, that's usually my ego trying to slip back into the driver's seat. So here's the rule I live by: I may not be able to stop all the chatter, but I certainly can decide what I listen to.

TAKING IT TO THE STREET

Summary: Park Your Ego

My ego has been driving my behavior for so long, there are times I can't even see when it's in charge. There I am, living my life, not even realizing that all of the overacting, muscle flexing, and posturing is nothing more than my ego trying to deal with everything that's being thrown at it. Don't get me wrong. My ego has protected me ever since I was a kid, all in an attempt to keep me safe. But I've also learned one very important lesson about ego: When it has me in a headlock, my options decrease and my garbage multiplies.

> WHEN EGO HAS ME IN A HEADLOCK, MY OPTIONS DECREASE AND MY GARBAGE MULTIPLIES.

The opposite side of my ego is the Inner Garbageman. He has a direct pipeline to the fearless side of me, the part that stares the unknown right in the eye and quietly says, "Bring it on." New? Unfamiliar? Way out of the comfort zone? Not a problem for the Inner Garbageman. He's trained to live there. And that's a neighborhood that the ego has never visited.

I know this sounds like some epic battle between good and evil. It's not. It's just two sides of my personality that each get behind the wheel and drive me through my life. At the end of the day though, I don't want my ego racking up the miles. It's too volatile, too influenced by emotion, and too quick to go to the old standard to solve problems. That usually brings me more drama and more chaos, which always leads to more garbage.

When I park my ego and let my Inner Garbageman drive, TBOs line up with my actions. I'm more consistent and more controlled, and I don't feel like a different person every other minute. In a world where I depend on other people and they depend on me, putting the Inner Garbageman in the driver's seat is the only way to go.

EXERCISES

1. **Which has more control over your life, your Inner Garbageman or your ego?**

_____

_____

_____

_____

_____

2. How often do you find confidence inside yourself, as opposed to finding it through reassurance from others? Are you happy with this balance? If not, what steps can you take to shift it?

_____

_____

_____

_____

_____

3. List the top five masks that you wear and the situations that cause you to put them on.

_____

_____

_____

_____

_____

4. How difficult is it for you to listen when you're in an argument with someone?

_____

_____

_____

_____

5. Make a list of the team members you have in your life. List
    the key areas where each helped you get rid of garbage that
    was weighing you down. Then, the next time you speak with
    them, let them know that you're grateful for the help they
    give you.

    _____

    _____

    _____

    _____

    _____

6. List five ways you can be more humble.

    _____

    _____

    _____

    _____

    _____

STEP 5
LEAVE IT IN THE LANDFILL

"To forgive is to set a prisoner free
and discover that the prisoner was you."
—Lewis B. Smedes

Every day, I drive to the landfill when my truck gets full. Even though I've been there a million times, the place never ceases to amaze me. Huge garbage mashers spread and compact the trash. Layers of fresh dirt cover the garbage. Trucks move in and out like clockwork and the whole place is extremely well run. This is no town dump. It's a modern, scientifically managed facility that's almost miraculous for being the final resting spot for trash.

There's something else I notice whenever I leave the landfill. I always see a couple of guys picking off bags and pieces of paper that are stuck to the fence. You see, it's pretty common for the wind to blow around some of the light garbage before it has a chance to be properly buried. If the landfill operator doesn't pick that trash off and put it back in the landfill, it can act like a sail, catching even more of the wind until it eventually knocks down the fence. Once that happens, the crew has to stop what they're doing, assess the damage, and make repairs. That means more time and energy taken away from what they need to do the most: manage the garbage that's being thrown out.

When I toss a TBO into my landfill, I don't expect it to pop into my head again. I assume that I'm done with it—and for the most part, I am. However, some TBOs keep coming back, over and over again, even though I've passed them through my Value Filter, declared them to be garbage, and dumped them two, three, and even four times.

That means the normal Step 1-2-3 cycle isn't working and there's a deeper reason why this particular piece of trash is sticking to me. To get rid of it, I have to find out why I'm maintaining a relationship with a thought that I labeled as garbage and attempted to throw out. If I don't dig deeper and I just let that TBO keep rolling around in my head, the winds of life will focus on that thought and eventually knock me to the ground, just like that fence. That's why I want to spend a chapter talking about how to handle old garbage that keeps blowing out of my landfill. Because learning how to control it gets me out of the dumps and keeps me focused on my life's route.

ABOUT MENTAL CONTRACTS

I think the reason why certain TBOs keep blowing out of my landfill is that I've made a mental contract with them that I can't break. Let me tell you what I mean by that.

I usually think of a contract as an agreement I make with another person. It always has two sides: something I give up and something I get, like giving up time to do a job in order to get money. I always thought of a contract as a grown-up thing, something I would enter into as an adult when I was old enough to sign my name on the dotted line.

When I look closer though, I can see that I've been making contracts ever since I was a kid—mostly with myself. When something bad happened, like the first time I got beat up, I wrote a mental contract with myself that said I'd fight back no matter what. When my favorite uncle died, I wrote a contract that said I'd tough it out and not show anyone how upset I was. I've kept these mental contracts in place for years, cementing them with some deeply held TBOs. And I'll be the first one to tell you that with some of these contracts, I gave a whole lot more than I ever got back.

> WITH SOME OF THESE CONTRACTS, I GAVE A WHOLE LOT MORE THAN I EVER GOT BACK.

I know people who have written some terrible contracts with themselves: bad marriages, lousy financial investments, or reactions to a traumatic event that they witnessed. Even though the balance between the give and take of those contracts was way off, their ego took over and wouldn't let them admit that they had made a mistake. So whether they created the scenario that led to the contract or it wandered into their life on its own, they become a victim to those contracts and wouldn't tear them up.

It's sad, but I've seen people do some horrific things when they're under the influence of a contract, harming themselves and others. At the end of the day, constantly living as a victim or in reaction to a lousy contract makes for a very unhappy life. I know that when my head is in that place, I'm usually miserable. And any TBO that I've linked to that contract will keep blowing out of my landfill, no matter how many times I bury it.

WHY TRASH COMES OUT OF THE LANDFILL

So here I am, going through my day, and a TBO pops into my mind. I run it through my Value Filter, decide that it's garbage, and throw it into my landfill—the mental equivalent of canceling the contract I had with it. At that point, I expect that I'll never see that TBO again.

Then, life happens.

All of a sudden, without any warning, I run headfirst into a situation that brings up old emotions and feelings. The next thing I know, that TBO I threw away works its way out of my landfill and sticks to me all over again. Any TBO hooked to that event (for example, *Nothing I plan ever works out*) gets a supercharge of emotion and I find myself right back at square one, re-engaging with a contract I thought I had torn up.

Why does this happen? Remember the concept of Trash Triggers that we talked about earlier? They are the biggest culprits. A Trash Trigger is any event or object or thought that triggers an emotional reaction that makes me start questioning my decision to throw away a TBO. I hear a song on the radio or catch a snippet of conversation and *bam!* The memories come flooding back again. There's no way I can change what happened, so my brain compensates by replaying the event over and over again, feelings and all, as if that's somehow going to make me feel better. I obsess about it, reliving every excruciating detail by pulling old TBOs out of my personal landfill. And if I'm already in a funk? Trash Triggers fire even easier.

What are your most common Trash Triggers?

Trash Triggers cause involuntary reactions, like the way my knee jerks when the doctor hits it with that little rubber hammer. I don't consciously say to myself, "Gee. I want to feel miserable today. I think I'll head over to my personal landfill and pull out some self-defeating TBOs." I just do it, as if some invisible force has taken over my power of reasoning and tells me to start second-guessing myself.

Trash Triggers can sneak up on me. For example, I'm helping a friend through a tough time and start to notice that his problem ever so slightly reminds me of one I used to have. Pretty soon, I find myself sinking into a funk. Or I'm at a family function and some tipsy in-law lets loose with a stream of criticisms about me—and I begin to believe what I hear. In both cases, I'm at my landfill, shovel in hand, digging out trash instead of using my broom to sweep it back in.

Here's what's so frustrating. The logical part of my brain knows that nothing will be accomplished by digging through my own personal garbage. Once the value is gone, it's not coming back. I mean, that's why I threw it out in the first place! But my feelings aren't logical. Once they've taken over, it's much easier for garbage to blow out of my landfill. That's when I get stuck in the past, revisiting old contracts that I've torn up and questioning whether I've done the right thing.

One last word. We all have trash that blows out of our landfill. Divorce, death, accidents, and injuries create scars that make it very difficult to separate us from our past. No matter how much mental trash we say we're tossing, trust me: old garbage sticks to all of us. So don't feel like you're the only one who gets hit by persistent TBOs. It's just part of life.

THE DANGER OF CLINGING TRASH

Taking action when old trash is clinging to me can be a very bad idea.

For starters, acting on ancient garbage in the heat of the moment can have some bad ramifications. Who knows how much damage I can do to a relationship or a job interview or an important negotiation while I'm standing in the middle of my personal landfill? If I'm obsessing about not repeating a past blunder instead of focusing on the person I'm trying to become, there's a good chance I'm going to make a boneheaded mistake in judgment.

Second, acting on persistent TBOs that keep blowing out of my landfill can reopen very old wounds. I have friends who have texted an old flame when a Trash Trigger fires, only to find themselves back in the same mess that led them to break up with the person in the first place. And I've found that getting out of the same situation a second time ends up being far more difficult than the first.

> ACTING ON PERSISTENT TBOs THAT KEEP BLOWING OUT OF MY LANDFILL CAN REOPEN VERY OLD WOUNDS.

Then, there's the longevity problem. Not putting stubborn garbage back in the landfill can keep issues alive forever. Take my uncle, for example. He had a nasty argument with one of his brothers when he was in his twenties and he didn't speak to him for decades after that. Imagine the energy it takes to hold on to that much anger! I often wonder what direction his life would have gone if he hadn't been burdened by all that weight. For me, I always pay a price when I carry a grudge.

Finally, letting old garbage that I've already dumped cling to me over and over again means I keep operating on really bad information. Listen, I formed most of my TBOs when I was a kid—good ones and bad ones. Back then, I had no clue about why people acted the way they did. I just took what was coming at me and made it up as I went. Sure, I had my moments—a few good decisions that make me say, "Man, I was pretty smart for being so young." For the most part though, my old TBOs were created out of fear of a world I didn't yet understand. And here I am—a grown adult—and I still hold on to those TBOs instead of putting them in my personal landfill. You know what that means? I'm essentially operating as an adult using badly outdated, highly inaccurate childhood reasoning. That won't get me very far, will it?

I had a friend whose first job out of college was with a big electronics company. He worked his tail off in that place. Yet, despite a never-ending stream of plaques, promotions, and pep talks, he couldn't get it through his head that he was doing a good job. He kept torpedoing himself at every opportunity, constantly tearing himself down and shrugging off any "attaboy" that came his way. No matter how much his colleagues tried to tell him that he was a good performer, he kept digging up *I'm not good enough.*

Eventually, his rise through the company began to slow. Because he kept telegraphing his lack of confidence in himself, people eventually got the message. Projects started to go to other managers. Committee assignments dried up. Executives began to focus on other up-and-comers. My friend still did a bang-up job for the company, but he never reached his full potential there because he couldn't find a way to pick off all that old garbage that kept sticking to him.

FORGIVENESS AND DUMPING PERSISTENT TBOs

So here I am, staring at a persistent TBO that keeps clinging to me. How do I put it back in the landfill—and leave it there for good? Here's my answer: *Break the bond with the event that had me create the TBO in the first place.* From everything I've learned, the only way for me to do that is through forgiveness.

Here's what I mean by that. Pretend someone wants to borrow five thousand dollars from me. I ask around for advice and am warned not to do business with this person because his credit history is shaky. I weigh the options, crunch some numbers, and decide to make the loan anyway. Nine months later, the person goes broke and files for bankruptcy, making the odds that the loan will ever be paid back slim to none. Now, all I have to show for my investment is a worthless loan contract and a bad debt. What now?

Well, I could spend a lot of time hand wringing and wailing about the stupid decision I made. I could kick myself for not listening to the advice I received. I could replay the scenario over and over again in my mind. I could focus on everything I'll miss out on because I lost the money. I'd do all of this with the hope that somehow getting all of this out of my system will make me feel better.

Or, I could forgive the loan. I could say to myself, "Look, I made a bad decision. I did the best I could at the time, but it didn't work out." I could rip up the loan contract because it's garbage. I could tell myself that I no longer have a connection to the debt. I could write off the whole situation, walk away, and start over again.

The second scenario is a perfect example of forgiveness and how it applies to mental garbage. Forgiveness is both the realization and the acceptance that the issue I'm turning over in my head no longer has any value, it's garbage, and it's time to let it go. It's recognizing that the same TBO is coming back again and again and the normal Step 1-2-3 cycle is not enough to get rid of it. It's a conscious choice to stop suffering and stop being victimized by a past event and all the TBOs that I've made up about it. Once I accept that, I can be more deliberate in putting all that garbage back in my landfill. Forgiveness lets me stop expecting something out of myself that will never happen: changing the events that led to the creation of this TBO. Forgiveness allows me to sever my connection with the event, tear up my contract with it, and walk away. The more I forgive, the better my chances that the garbage TBO will stay in my landfill for good.

FORGIVENESS IS A CONSCIOUS CHOICE TO STOP SUFFERING.

Part of forgiveness is taking a long, hard look at the contract I have with a persistent TBO. I need to challenge myself by asking why I still keep interacting with it after I already decided it was garbage and I threw it into my landfill. I need to look at the payoff I'm getting and compare that to what it's costing me to keep investing in it. That will tell me if I really think this TBO is garbage. If I decide—again—that it's trash, I can use forgiveness to help me take another shot at putting the TBO back in my landfill. That's what it means to take control of my tougher, more difficult-to-toss garbage. At some point, if I want to become a different person, I have to look through my life and examine the contracts I've put in place.

Over the years, I've become an expert at beating myself up when a situation goes sideways. By continually letting the same TBO come out of the landfill and roll around in my head, I'm prolonging that beating—and that has to stop if I'm going to get on with my life. Forgiveness lets me say, "Look, I did the best I could back then. Shredding myself is not going to change what happened." When I think about it like that, I begin to set the stage to put the persistent TBO back in the landfill—and leave it there.

Sometimes, I feel bad about permanently tossing a TBO in my landfill—which could be a reason it keeps blowing out. Maybe it involves someone I used to be very close with. Maybe it deals with a painful loss or a time I was taken advantage of by someone I trusted. But at some point, I have to stop walking around with all these bad contracts by forgiving them and moving on. Otherwise, it's like being tied to a post in the middle of my past. There's nowhere for me to go!

Don't get me wrong. Forgiveness is not an excuse. If I made a mess of things, I still need to clean it up. At the same time, forgiveness lets me stop shredding myself for not being a perfect human being. Look, all I have is this moment, right now—and I don't want to water it down by kicking myself about what could have been. Forgiveness is a separation between the past and the present, a way to say that I'm no longer going to mix the two anymore. It lets me get this monkey called *I had a lousy experience* off my back. Because frankly, I get tired of carrying it around all the time—especially if I try to let it go and it keeps coming back over and over again.

At the same time, forgiveness never means that I have to excuse what the other person did. If there were consequences for him because of what happened, forgiveness doesn't interfere with or change that. I also don't need to have contact with the other person to forgive, which is great if he did something really bad and I don't want to deal with him anymore. Forgiveness doesn't mean I have to forget or explain away what happened. It's just a way to tell myself, "Come on! Leave the pain, guilt, and regret over what happened in the landfill. All that stuff is garbage and it's time to let it all go and get on with life."

Have you ever forgiven like we're discussing here? What happened? What process did you use to forgive? How did you feel afterwards?

Forgiveness is not the same as an apology. I don't say, "Once you apologize to me for what you did, I will forgive you." All that does is keep the conflict alive and cement the two of us in our "I'm right and you're wrong" positions. Forgiveness has nothing to do with the other person at all. It is solely and strictly my choice to move beyond the situation so it's not running me over anymore.

Here's a great way to think about forgiveness. When I was a teenager, the kid next door invited me to play basketball with him. During the game, he asked me about the comings and goings of our family, which I told him, not thinking anything of it. A week later, I came home from school and found a couple of police cars parked in front of our house. Someone had broken in and robbed us.

Now, flash forward about thirty years. My whole family was sitting around the Thanksgiving table, telling stories about growing up, when my sister brought up the robbery. *Bam!* Before I knew what hit me, the guilt and the embarrassment were right back in my face again. My dad noticed that I looked upset, and he asked me what was wrong. When I told him, his jaw dropped—along with everyone else's at the table. He couldn't believe that I still felt bad about what had happened. He asked me why I never said anything before, but I couldn't answer him. All I could think about was how my sister lost her favorite necklace and how my dad lost the pocket watch my grandpa had given to him. There I was, a fully-grown man feeling like a shamefaced fifteen-year-old kid again.

"Don't you realize that the neighbor kid pumped you for information?" my dad said. "For crying out loud, you thought he was your friend. How could you know what he was doing?" Then, everyone else jumped in, telling me over and over again that it wasn't my fault. It took a while, but I finally let go of the thirty-year-old TBO that I was to blame for the robbery. And let me tell you, if I hadn't done that, I would have dragged that ball and chain around for another thirty years.

THE BENEFITS OF FORGIVENESS

Forgiveness is a huge mindset shift that's day and night from constantly beating myself up about a certain part of my past. When I forgive, I'm not a person who's vindictive and blames others and myself for the way things turned out. I don't feel cheated and resentful, nor do I walk around with a dark gray cloud hanging over my head. Instead, forgiveness frees me to spend my time looking forward, not back. It gives me the control and focus I need to *make* things different, rather than *wish* that they were different. It lets me say, "I'm tired of dealing with the same garbage all the time. I'm putting this trash back where it belongs: in my landfill."

> FORGIVENESS FREES ME TO SPEND MY TIME LOOKING FORWARD, NOT BACK.

Here are a few other benefits of forgiveness:

- I can stop my brain from asking "What if?" all the time.

- I can honor my past without obsessing over it.

- I get some closure.

- I can move on to TBOs that have positive, lasting value to me.

- I just feel better because I'm not being hounded by the same old TBOs all the time.

- I get out of the dumps.

- I can create an Empty Zone in the spot where the persistent garbage used to keep distracting me. That gives me a huge opportunity to clear my mind and steer my thoughts in a whole new direction.

Finally, forgiveness works for me because of its simplicity: Let go of the past and get some relief in the present.

THE LANDFILL MANAGEMENT PROGRAM

Every landfill needs management—including the one I've created in my mind. If my goal is to keep trash in there, I have to be ready when life blows it back on me. That's what the Landfill Management Program does. It gives me some definitive steps I can take to keep the garbage where it belongs: in my past.

1. **Identify the mental contracts that I've linked to persistent TBOs.**

   If I'm going to stop beating myself up with the same garbage over and over again, the first step is to pay closer attention to what I'm thinking and feeling. Do I clam up every time I hear a Beatles song or do I go negative every time I see a certain person in the office? That kind of recurring garbage may be hooked to an old contract that I need to pull up and examine—especially if a Trash Trigger brings it up time after time.

I have found that keeping a list of the mental contracts I uncover is really useful. If I notice myself feeling a certain way or thinking certain thoughts over and over again, I write them down. Looking at them in this kind of cold, objective light really helps start me down the path of breaking my bond with especially tough TBOs that I've created so I can dump them in my landfill.

2. Run the persistent TBO through an enhanced Value Filter.

Let's say I uncover a contract with a stubborn TBO that keeps sticking to me. It's clear that my regular Value Filter isn't enough to hold it in the landfill because, if it were, I'd see that the TBO had no value and I'd leave it alone. That's why I need an enhanced Value Filter, one that works harder to show me the uselessness of the TBO and how much it's knocking me down every time I let it stick to me.

An enhanced Value Filter uses even tougher criteria to determine if a TBO has value. Here's a short list of the criteria I use:

- What's the real payoff I keep getting when I allow this garbage to constantly blow out of the landfill? Am I manipulating that payoff so I can get what I want?

- How much is this contract really costing me in terms of time, money, and energy? And how much of that is a complete waste? Will I ever get a high enough return to make it worthwhile? If it's a big waste with a lousy return, then why do I keep investing in it?

- Is chewing on the same TBO over and over getting me anywhere? At the end of the day, am I playing small and giving in to this garbage?

- What if I stay in the contract for another year? Five years? Ten years? How will my life look if I'm still hounded by the same garbage for that long?

If I'm letting the same TBO stick to me over and over again, I must have rediscovered some value in it—which means it's really not garbage anymore. An enhanced Value Filter forces me to take a second look at the TBO and be brutally honest with myself. It's tough, I'll admit—but so is the TBO. If I really want it out of my life, I have to accept that it truly is garbage. Asking hard, no-nonsense questions is a great way to do that.

3.   **Initiate a Forgiveness Cycle.**

If I decide the contract with the persistent TBO is trash, then breaking the bond I have with it is the best way to stop it from blowing out of the landfill. The most effective tool I know of to do that is the Forgiveness Cycle. Here's how it works.

I relive the experience. When a memory keeps swallowing me up over and over again, I step back and imagine that I'm watching what happened on a huge movie screen. This gives me some distance from the event—almost like it involved someone else, not me.

I forgive myself for my role in what happened. Sometimes, I'll say the words "I forgive myself" out loud. Other times, I'll just think them or write them down. But I make sure they consciously pass through my brain. Listen, if I'm condemning myself because of what I did or did not do, telling myself that I'm forgiven is a great way to stop that.

I tell myself, "I'm done with this. I'm not willing to give it any more energy." This is where I tear up the contract in my head. Saying that I'm done being eaten alive by a past TBO stops it dead in its tracks, like killing power to my truck. It might come back later, but I don't care. All I want is relief right now. And ripping up a useless contract is a great way to free my mind from garbage so I can concentrate on something else.

Create a ritual or symbolic act. If I think it will help, sometimes I'll end my Forgiveness Cycle with a ritual. I'll write down what happened on a piece of paper and tear it up like I would a dead contract. Or I may call a buddy and talk it out with him. Heck, my wife's friend ties it to the end of a helium balloon and lets it go. It doesn't matter what the ritual is, as long as it stops the suffering and lets me move on from what happened.

My friend Mark served in the military. He had completed some basic courses and was scheduled to attend flight school and become a pilot. That would have given him a ton of prestige, a good-paying job, and the chance to pursue flying, which he really loved. It was also what his father expected him to do. And if you knew Mark's dad, you did not want to disappoint him.

Unfortunately, with some of the foreign entanglements our country was in at the time, there was a possibility that Mark would end up a wartime pilot. He was afraid that military combat would fundamentally change who he was—a risk he was unwilling to take given his deep moral and spiritual convictions. So he decided instead to combine his two other passions—art and teaching—and to become a high school art instructor.

Needless to say, Mark's father was extremely unhappy. He had very different expectations for his son's career, and teaching a bunch of teenagers to draw was not one of them. Though Mark loved what he did, he never let go of the old negative TBOs that told him he had made the wrong career choice. He'd watch a TV show about a pilot or he'd fly somewhere and the same feelings of regret would come up over and over again. I know it stole some of the joy out of his teaching.

Over time, Mark got tired of feeling this way, so he started experimenting with Forgiveness Cycles whenever his *bad career choice* TBOs took over. Eventually, he saw that what he had gained as an art teacher was far more valuable than what he had lost by not being a pilot. It took him a while, but eventually, Mark let go of the *bad career choice* garbage. Guess what happened after that? His love of teaching went off the scale.

4. If it's appropriate, take action.

Sometimes, my Forgiveness Cycle turns up some actions I can take that can bring me even more relief from my recurring TBOs. If it feels like the right thing to do, I write a letter. I clear the air. I do whatever I need to bring me closure, so long as it comes from my heart and it doesn't hurt anyone else.

What I try not to do is attach any expectations to my actions—for example, promise myself that everything will be rosy again if I just have a conversation with the other person. Expectations like that will just set me up for more disappointment. I try to keep my actions focused solely on the goal of closing the chapter and moving on.

5. Remember that forgiveness, like emptying garbage, is a process and not an event.

It doesn't surprise me that I may need a few Forgiveness Cycles to get some of my persistent garbage under control. Depending on the size and emotional charge of the TBO, a day or a week or a month from now, I may yank the same event right back out of my personal landfill. If this happens, all I need to do is repeat the Forgiveness Cycle. That helps me put the TBO back down in my landfill and keep any Empty Zones I created free from old, useless trash.

> REMEMBER THAT FORGIVENESS, LIKE EMPTYING GARBAGE, IS A PROCESS AND NOT AN EVENT.

The more I do this, the less intense the TBO will be if it blows out again. If this is my third or fourth go-around, I may not need a full Forgiveness Cycle. It might be as simple as, "Hey. I already let that go a few times before. I'm done with it." Sounds a lot like how I toss lighter-weight TBOs, doesn't it? That's the long-term beauty of forgiveness: The more I do it, the more of the event I can leave in the landfill—permanently.

Forgiving old TBOs that keep blowing out of my landfill can be very, very powerful. My wife has a dear friend who was sexually abused when he was a kid. I can't begin to tell you how much trauma that caused him. He had serious issues with intimacy. He had problems with authority figures. And to make matters worse, he often turned to alcohol to deaden his feelings.

There's no way anyone can wipe away the trauma of what happened. He was a helpless little kid taken advantage of by a sick, twisted adult. At the same time, my wife's friend had a choice. He could continue to be victimized by the abuse and let it completely define him as a person. Or he could make the decision to stop letting his past, with all of its garbage, stand in the way of his future. And that's exactly what he chose to do.

Thanks to some great work he did with a professional counselor, he began to see how deep his contract with the abuse ran. He started examining the effect the abuse had on him, how he kept it alive in his mind for so long, and how much it was costing him every single day of his life. He began pulling away from the event by writing down his thoughts and feelings about what happened, then symbolically burning it like you would a contract that is no longer in force. He stopped blaming himself for the fact that as a ten-year-old kid, he couldn't find a way to end the abuse.

THAT'S THE POWER OF ENDING THE CONTRACT: PEACE, CLOSURE, AND A NEW BEGINNING.

Gradually, he chipped away at this huge, life-altering event, throwing away one piece of garbage, then two, then three, until the pile of TBOs he had created around it began to shrink. Slowly, he began rewriting the contract he had with that part of his life. Today, he's a different person, focused on where he wants to go, rather than frozen where he had been. That's the power of ending the contract: peace, closure, and a new beginning.

USE CAUTION

These are items I look out for when I'm working with trash that keeps blowing out of my landfill.

Don't Rush the Process

If the goal is to dump the thoughts and opinions that keep blowing out of my personal landfill, I first have to drive through the gates of forgiveness to get there. That means I have to take the time to run through the steps in the Landfill Management Plan if I truly want to be free of the garbage.

Instead of running a persistent thought or belief through a Forgiveness Cycle, I sometimes just dismiss it again with a quick "Never mind" or an off-the-cuff "That's stupid," as if I'm throwing out a lightweight TBO. Skimming over the top of blown-back garbage is really easy to do when I'm face-to-face with an emotionally charged TBO that makes me uncomfortable, and I know that digging into it is going to stir up a hornet's nest of feelings.

If I rush the Landfill Management Plan, I won't be truly free of the garbage that keeps bothering me. It'll keep reminding me of some past event that I don't like and continue to pull me off my route and onto some unproductive side trip. That's why rushing is never as good as forgiving. It makes me feel better in the short term, but over time it just keeps my old mess alive.

Don't Play the Blame Game

My relationships can really take it on the chin when I don't forgive. If I keep blaming myself for what happened, in all likelihood I'm probably blaming other people, too. And that doesn't count all those unresolved feelings like anger and resentment that love to hover around old

> MY RELATIONSHIPS CAN REALLY TAKE IT ON THE CHIN WHEN I DON'T FORGIVE.

garbage that's blown out of my landfill. Eventually, all that energy is going to leak into the way I'm interacting with people, and that's a scenario I'd really like to avoid.

As I filter the thoughts streaming through my head, I try and look for any that involve blame. If I find them, there's a good chance they're hooked to some old garbage that's sticking to me—and that's an opportunity to tear up some contracts and start over again.

PUT OUT YOUR RECYCLING

If there was ever a time to discuss recycling, it's now.

Sometimes, if an old TBO has blown out of the landfill and is sticking to me, I find it tough to put it back there, even after going through a Forgiveness Cycle. If I hit one of those, I try a different approach: recycling it into something new. For example:

GARBAGE THOUGHT (NO VALUE)	RECYCLED THOUGHT (HAS VALUE)
"I'll never figure out a way to get this project off the ground."	"What if I approached it from this new angle…"
"I'm too out of shape to do that 10K run everyone's talking about."	"If I start training this week, I'll bet I could be ready by race day."
"There's no way I have the qualifications to apply for that job."	"When I think about it, I have a lot more experience than I realized."

This kind of thought recycling can be the perfect way to manage garbage that just won't leave me alone. Listen, the whole concept of *The Garbageman's Guide to Life* is to shift my thinking and push my mind to deal with my past in a whole new light. For some garbage that won't stay in the landfill, recycling thoughts does exactly that.

TAKING IT TO THE STREET

SUMMARY: LEAVE IT IN THE LANDFILL

When a TBO pops into my head and my Value Filter tells me that it's garbage, I toss it right into my landfill. Most of the time, I never hear from that TBO again, which is how the normal Step 1-2-3 cycle works. Every once in a while though, I'll notice that the same TBO will cross my mind again and again. Maybe a Trash Trigger shook loose a memory. Or maybe I'm facing a difficult situation that's flooding me with old familiar feelings. Whatever the case, I need to take a closer look at why this TBO keeps blowing out of my landfill.

To do this, I examine the mental contract I drew up during the events that created the TBO. What do I get from continuing the contract? What is it costing me? Is this contract moving me further along my route, or is it hurting me in the long run? Then, I run the persistent TBO past an enhanced Value Filter and decide if it's garbage. If I arrive at the same conclusion—this really is trash and my initial decision to toss it was the right one—then I need a stronger tool to put it back in my landfill and keep it there. I use forgiveness to help me do that.

Forgiveness is a deliberate set of steps designed to break the bond I have with a TBO and the events that created it. I use a Forgiveness Cycle to sever that relationship. Forgiveness lets me tear up the contract I created with the TBO and throw it into the landfill again. By giving persistent thoughts and beliefs this kind of focused attention, I can chip away at the power they exert over me and cut down how often they pop out of the landfill—until eventually, they stay there for good.

> FORGIVENESS LETS ME TEAR UP THE CONTRACT I CREATED WITH THE TBO AND THROW IT INTO THE LANDFILL AGAIN

EXERCISES

1. Look through your mind and find a piece of mental garbage that keeps blowing out of your landfill. Write it down below.

_____

_____

_____

_____

_____

2. What have you done in the past when this garbage sticks to you? Does it hit you just as strongly each time it reappears?

_____

_____

_____

_____

_____

3. What would you have to do to break your bond with the event? Write it down below, and then do it.

_____

_____

_____

_____

_____

4. Go through a Forgiveness Cycle for the event.

_____

_____

_____

_____

_____

5. As you look at the event, how attached do you feel to it now?
    How do you think you'll feel the next time it blows out of the
    landfill?

_____

_____

_____

_____

_____

STEP 6
GET AWAY FROM TOXIC WASTE

"There is no waste more toxic than potential squandered and dreams unfulfilled."
—Anonymous

I had been on the job for just a few months, still learning the ins and outs of hauling trash, when halfway through my route I noticed a terrible smell coming from the back of my truck. All of a sudden, it was hard to breathe, I started wheezing, and my eyes felt like they were on fire. What happened next was nothing short of amazing.

When I radioed in, the dispatcher calmly asked me a series of very specific questions. A few minutes later, emergency vehicles arrived. A policeman cordoned off an area around my truck to keep folks away. Three people in protective suits went to work on the trash I was hauling. A paramedic helped me get my breathing under control again. There was no panic or drama, just a group of professionals who appeared on the scene and got to work.

It turns out that someone along my route had dropped some half-empty bottles of hot tub chemicals into his trash can. Somehow, they had mixed with water, soda, and other liquids in the back of my truck, forming a dangerous cloud of chlorine gas. What started out as low-level toxic waste—those hot tub chemicals—had morphed into a high-level toxic mess that took the pros and their unique skills a lot of time and effort to contain and clean up.

If I were to take what happened and apply it to what's going on inside of my head, I'd see that mental garbage is not created equally. Some of the TBOs I'm carrying around are really toxic and self-destructive. If I combine those with hazardous relationships or poisonous situations, I have the possibility of creating a real toxic mess that can have some very bad side effects.

I'd also see how much easier things go when the pros get involved. Judging by the way they jumped into action, I could have sworn the team who helped me had been working together for fifty years. It made me realize that when I don't have the know-how to manage a mess that I'm in, the best thing I can do is get out of the way and let the professionals handle it—especially when it involves something as risky as toxic waste.

Garbage companies have done an incredible job managing all kinds of trash—including toxic waste. Over the years, they've developed amazing equipment, procedures, and know-how to keep trash safe and protect the environment at the same time. The exact same thing happened with me as I learned to deal with my own mental garbage. The more I became aware of toxic waste in my life, the more I developed really good techniques that helped protect me from it.

Toxic waste is not everyday garbage. It needs special care and special handling. And because I don't see it very often, it's easy to miss it or get caught off-guard when it shows up. That's why this chapter is a little different from the others. Not only will I be focusing on the toxic waste

TOXIC WASTE IS NOT EVERYDAY GARBAGE.

that I make, I'll be talking about the toxic waste that comes from other people, too.

Listen, this stuff is dangerous. It's unsafe. Long-term exposure depletes my energy and enthusiasm and is absolutely deadly to my route and to the goals I set for myself. So here's everything I know about emotional toxic waste. Because at the end of the day, no one deserves to be exposed to this kind of garbage.

LOW-LEVEL TOXIC WASTE

There are two type of toxic waste: low-level and high-level. Low-level toxic waste is like bleach or Drano or weed killer. I know they're hazardous, but I've been around them for a long time and I have some experience dealing with them. There's usually a warning label on the back that tells me how to use it, how to handle it without getting hurt, and how to get rid of it safely. In small doses, it's not that dangerous to be around low-level toxic waste as long as I protect myself.

Low-level toxic waste needs special handling because it can easily affect my behavior if I mishandle it. It contains poisonous by-products like old festering memories or strong unresolved feelings, so it can't go in the landfill with my regular garbage. If I ignore the fact that it's toxic and treat it like normal trash, there's a good chance I'll get contaminated.

Just because a TBO is negative doesn't mean it's toxic. A belief like *I'll never get promoted* may skew the way I look at the world, but the damage it does to my psyche is somewhat limited. It's regular garbage and I have tools like my Value Filter and the landfill to help me get rid of it.

Here are some examples of low-level toxic waste. As you can see, it's not everyday, run-of-the-mill mental garbage. This stuff needs special handling.

- **Taking a spouse for granted.** It's so easy for me to discount my wife and everything that she does for our family and for me. I nitpick stupid things. I get lazy and stop being attentive. I let our sex life drift. I expect her to keep things running smoothly instead of thanking her for it. Over time, the toxicity of taking her for granted chips away at our intimacy and weakens our marriage.

- **Second-rate treatment.** A co-worker or a family member is jealous of me and cuts me down to size whenever we meet. (To make it worse, we work together or we're related.) These are the people who come with a warning label. If I treat them like anyone else in my life—that is, with no special handling—I guarantee I'm going to get burned by them. For example, if a person at work is jealous of me and I don't treat him as toxic in my mind, he could seriously wreck my career.

Here are some examples of situations that can turn into low-level toxic waste. These aren't toxic in and of themselves. However, if I add the right mix of negative TBOs to them, I could have a real mess on my hands.

- **The company holiday party.** Not having a plan for the party can lead to drinking too much and making an idiot out of myself in front of everyone—two toxic situations I'd much rather avoid.

- **Family functions.** I walk in with expectations that everything is going to be great—and I get caught completely off guard when all the old stuff like childhood resentments and simmering arguments get dredged up. That makes it even harder for our family to stop arguing and get along.

- **Credit cards.** Credit cards come with a big warning label: those multipage agreements with the tiny mouseprint. The reason they can be so toxic is that I could use them to buy stuff I can't really afford and end up creating a huge toxic debt with a really high interest rate. That would destroy so many future opportunities because all my energy and money would be going to service that debt.

Low-level toxic thoughts and hazardous relationships usually contain remnants of old, unresolved TBOs that just sit there and fester. That's what makes them so hazardous. Over the years, my brain keeps turning them over, adding layer after layer of emotion that raises their mental radioactivity. Then, something happens, and *boom!* They slingshot to the surface and contaminate everything around them. That's what creates the toxic mess—not only the waste, but also the aftermath of all the pollution that is created, like a discussion that blows into a huge argument, complete with angry, vicious words that I can never take back.

Low-level toxic waste can also be the by-product of bad behavior or bad handling of a person or a situation. When actions go sideways, the residue that's left behind can be very toxic: sharp feelings like irritation and bitterness or unresolved circumstances that smolder inside for a long time. This creates what I call *looping thoughts*: toxic TBOs that just sit there in my mind, churning over and over again to the point where nothing new can work its way in. It's as if my brain has downloaded a computer virus and it's caught in an infinite loop, obsessed with nothing but the same set of negative TBOs. Put the right combination together—a snarky email and an unsettled disagreement about who botched a customer project—and things can turn hazardous very quickly.

What's toxic in your life? How long has it been with you? What have the long-term consequences been?

Low-level toxic waste can change over time. Years ago, for example, I used to clean my tools with gasoline. It was only later, when some of my buddies got sick from lead poisoning, that I realized this was a toxic activity. Just like I know today not to dump motor oil down the drain anymore, I have to accept the fact that something that's valuable one day might end up being low-level toxic waste the next. When that happens, I need a plan to understand the risks I'm facing so I don't get contaminated. (More on the specifics of how to do this a little later.)

To protect myself from low-level toxic waste, I usually need a moderate amount of protection, the mental equivalent of thick rubber gloves or a pair of safety glasses. I need to be cautious, but not paranoid. I'm probably not going to die from low-level toxic waste, but it can do some real damage if I'm sloppy with it.

I also have to keep myself on a very tight leash. I'm not afraid to use weed killer in the yard or unclog a drain with a gallon of chemical drain cleaner. I'm used to working with these products, just like I'm used to small doses of toxic TBOs, whether they come from me or from other people. Here's the problem. It's easy for me to get overconfident and think, "Hey, if I can handle low-level toxic waste this well, I'm sure I can handle the more dangerous stuff." That's when I get myself into big trouble.

HIGH-LEVEL TOXIC WASTE

In the real world, high-level toxic waste is usually the by-product of an industrial process like mining or manufacturing. It contains nasty elements: mercury, heavy metals, and dangerous chemicals. It can cause cancer, pollute groundwater, and destroy wildlife. I'm not kidding when I say this is really bad stuff.

The mental equivalent of high-level toxic waste is just as corrosive. I'm talking about drug problems. Anger management issues. Obsessive/compulsive disorders. Abusive relationships. Some of these may be inside me or they may come from people I know or situations I find myself in. Either way, high-level toxic waste situations all have some basic characteristics that I can pick out:

- The amount of contamination that they spread gets worse over time.

- The person who's creating the high-level toxic waste (myself included) always seems to have an excuse to dump it on someone else.

- After a while, it defines the person. Other people begin to think of that person only in the context of his or her high-level toxic waste problem.

- The person with the high-level toxic waste ends up having the same conversations over and over again—and the conversations are almost always about the high-level toxic waste.

- The contamination spreads to the point where the person with the high-level toxic waste ends up alone and isolated.

- People dealing with high-level toxic waste generally won't seek help until they hit bottom.

- It takes a pretty big intervention in order to clean it up.

Look, it's a tough world out there. Financial pressure, raising a family, performing well on the job: it takes a thick skin and a lot of guts to slog through life, day in and day out. For some people, it's too much and they develop toxic waste shortcuts to help them cope. They'll hit their kids as a way of controlling them. They'll backstab and lie in order to get a promotion. This is the dark side of garbage, the evil trash that can do a lot of damage if it's not dealt with properly. It's not fun to talk about, but it can't be ignored if the goal is to have a balanced, healthy life. And here's one lesson I've learned about high-level toxic waste: there are always consequences if I ignore it.

Identifying high-level toxic waste can be tricky. People who are contaminated by it don't like to admit that they have a problem. That means I have to read the little clues to see how badly they're affected: personality quirks, weird things they might say, or facts that just don't add up. At the same time, I have to walk the line between vigilance and paranoia. Just like I don't call the fire department every time I see someone light a match, I don't want to overreact every time I see some unusual behavior. That's where working with professionals can help. They're going to read the tea leaves a whole lot better than I will and can help steer me in the right direction so I handle the situation correctly.

Here's the other tricky part about high-level toxic waste. I hate to see another person suffer. My first instinct is to jump in and help. However, rushing in and trying to fix everything without a plan is like pouring water on a grease fire: It usually makes the problem worse. Keeping my emotions in check is absolutely critical when handling high-level toxic waste—especially when it involves someone I really care about.

High-level toxic waste requires a serious amount of protection. In the case of my chlorine leak, the cleanup crew wore full hazmat suits, complete with respirators and protective body gear. The goal was full isolation, so they minimized the chances of contamination. I've developed the mental equivalent of a hazmat suit to keep myself from being affected by what's going on around me.

> HIGH-LEVEL TOXIC WASTE REQUIRES A SERIOUS AMOUNT OF PROTECTION.

The most important piece of that suit is recognizing that high-level toxic waste demands a skill set that I don't have. I need the pros like counselors or social workers to help me here. These are people with way more experience than I'll ever hope to have in dealing with this kind of hazardous waste. I don't go near it, I don't try to fix it, and I don't try to clean it up. I seek out the professionals and let them handle it. If it's appropriate, I'll monitor what's going on, but I won't jump in unless I'm specifically told what to do.

WHERE DOES TOXIC WASTE COME FROM?

Sometimes, it's easy to spot toxic waste, whether it's low-level or high-level. For example, I know who the office gossip is, or with a little research, those folks who are unethical in their business dealings. I'm going to stay as far away from those toxic relationships as I can.

Other times, situations turn toxic on their own. I know folks whose company had a change in management and now they hate working there. Or I've had friendships that started out great, but over time became so high maintenance that they weren't worth the effort I was putting into them. And I'm not blameless, either. I'll say or do something and be completely oblivious to the fact that it was toxic to another person.

Sometimes, I have to deal with toxic waste even when I try to avoid it. One of the best examples was a cousin of mine who was trustee of his mother's estate. Talk about a toxic situation! It turns out that when she was sick and he had power of attorney, he was paying himself a good chunk of change for managing her affairs. He then had her will changed so he'd get extra money just because he was the oldest son. He took over her investments and lost a bunch of money, which reduced the overall size of the estate and left less for his brothers and sisters. What I learned is that when it came to money, my cousin was extremely toxic. From that moment forward, I was very careful when dealing with him in any matter that involved family finances.

> SOMETIMES, I HAVE TO DEAL WITH TOXIC WASTE EVEN WHEN I TRY TO AVOID IT.

Part of the problem with toxic waste is that it's so much easier to run into it these days. Think about it. A hundred years ago, there was no email, texting, Skype, or Facebook. People either met face-to-face or wrote each other letters. These days, I'm hammered from all sides by tweets and wall posts. Plus, social media makes it really easy for people to dump their toxic TBOs for everyone to see. The sheer volume of input makes it so much more likely that one of these interactions is going to turn toxic. Add to that the fact that I'm a lot older now and I bring my entire history to every interaction I have. Some of that isn't pretty, increasing the chances that things can go sideways.

No matter where it comes from, when I stumble across a toxic TBO or a toxic situation, it's really important that I take decisive action. The last thing I want is to be around it for a long period of time, wondering what I should do instead of getting away from it.

VICTIM?

There's one more downside to toxic waste. It's called a victim mentality, and it's a killer.

When I come into contact with toxic waste, I get this feeling of powerlessness. Any forward momentum I had grinds to a halt and this defensive, *hold your ground* mindset takes over my brain. I feel like I have one hand on the trigger and the other on the doorknob, ready to fight or bolt at a moment's notice. It's like the world is conspiring against me and there's nothing I can do to stop it.

Here's the truth. I'm never going to get through my route when I'm a victim. Sure, I can park my truck on

Where are the places in your life that you're a victim? What steps can you take to break out of this role?

the side of the road, hoping that life will somehow get safer. But I'm going to be waiting there a long, long time. It's a tough world, and there's garbage all over the place. Acting like I'm a victim of it all does absolutely nothing except make me weak and useless.

I remember taking one of those courses on how to improve yourself. The instructor asked us to tell a story of a time when we felt like a victim and we'd all vote on the best one.

I thought I had this nailed. About a week before the class, someone had keyed my car—a big, ugly scratch from the front fender all the way to the back door. I had to fight the insurance company (originally, they didn't want to pay without jacking up my rates) and I ended up footing the bill for a really expensive paint job that I couldn't afford. I got up and told my story to the class, convinced that they would think I had every right to feel victimized.

Then, this woman stands up and tells us that her parents had died, she had moved to Seattle with her husband, gotten pregnant, and then had to fend for herself when her husband ran away with her sister (her only living relative), leaving her penniless and alone. She said that she was devastated and wallowed in a victim mentality for the longest time. Then, one day, she said to herself, "I'm done with this." She stopped feeling sorry for herself and took action. Today, she's a district manager for a food distribution company, her daughter is thriving, and she's dating a really nice guy.

Bam! It was like someone had thrown a bucket of ice water on me. All at once, I saw that my victim story was puny and insignificant. It also hit me that the keying of my car wasn't toxic. It was the way I had let my poor-me victim act get completely out of control. That's when I realized just how hazardous and unhealthy a victim mentality can really be.

A TOXIC-FREE LIFE

Despite its risks, I can stop toxic waste from contaminating my life once I come in contact with it. This kind of hazardous trash doesn't have to pollute my relationships or destroy my beliefs. Whether I'm creating it or I see it coming at me from someone else, recognizing toxic waste lets me jump into action and get out of its way. That means that in the long run, I'm going to be a whole lot healthier.

Sidestepping toxic waste also lets me take my power back. Getting out of a victim mentality means I keep my forward momentum and stay on track to the route I want for myself. *I'm* in control of my life, not the story about something that happened to me. I'm not saying that the event isn't important. It's part of what makes me who I am. However, having a plan whenever I run into toxic waste keeps that event in perspective so it doesn't take over my life anymore. Look, I have a lot of big dreams. The last thing I want is to have them taken off the field by a pile of toxic waste.

> SIDESTEPPING TOXIC WASTE ALSO LETS ME TAKE MY POWER BACK.

Getting rid of this kind of garbage also gives fear a swift kick in the rump. I love it when I'm no longer afraid of someone who's toxic or I can confront an emotionally hazardous situation and not be worried about it. Having a plan for dealing with toxic waste takes all the fear away, kind of like reading the label on the back of a bottle of pesticide. I know what to do, what to watch out for, and the role I can play in order to keep things safe.

A toxic-free life saves me hours of time. If I'm not obsessing over a toxic issue, my brain stops gravitating toward it and moves on to much bigger and better things. I can't begin to tell you how wonderful this is! It's as if someone opened my head and took out a huge, heavy weight from inside. It's the best feeling, especially when I know that I'm not going to chew up hours worrying about a toxic situation that has me in knots.

One of the best benefits of protecting myself from toxic waste is that sense of being even-keeled. I don't overreact and I don't underreact to it. I'm ready for it, secure in the knowledge that it won't pull me in and contaminate me.

Here's a great story about the power of managing toxic waste. Before I became a driver, I worked in an office and was putting in what seemed like a million hours a week to help the company through a really tough time. One day, the president burst into a meeting I was in and started bawling me out in front of everyone, complaining that things weren't getting done and that it was all my fault. When he was finished, he stormed out of the conference room and slammed the door behind him.

I remember sitting at that table, stunned, trying to process what had just happened. Normally, I would have taken that kind of abuse. My self-confidence was pretty low back then, and I used to think that if I got chewed out, I must have done something to deserve it. But not this time. Not with how hard I was working and how much I was giving to this little company. I quietly folded my notebook, stood up from the table, and walked straight to his office. I told him that if he ever talked to me like that again, I would quit on the spot and that would be the last he'd ever see of me. I then got in my car and took off the rest of the day.

The next morning, he called me into his office and profusely apologized for what he did. Hearing those words was like getting a medal. Until that point, I had never protected myself from someone else's high-level toxic waste. I felt a sense of power inside of me that was completely foreign—not an arrogant *I'm better than you* feeling, but rather the quiet satisfaction of knowing that I now had the tools to take care of myself whenever I ran into a pile of toxic waste. And life has been much better since.

TOXIC WASTE ACTION PLAN

To avoid getting hurt by toxic waste, I need to have a strategy in place, either before I run into it or as soon as I find that it's snuck up on me. That's what the Toxic Waste Action Plan does. It lets me respond automatically when I find myself face-to-face with the worst emotional garbage, whether it's mine or it belongs to someone else.

1. Practice the drill.

Preparing myself to go face-to-face with toxic waste starts with being realistic about all the places I know it's likely to show up. For example, there's a lady who lives on East Twenty-third Street who has a bunch of cats. When I empty her trash into the back of the truck, I know to hold my breath and turn my head or I'm going to get a mouthful of kitty litter dust. It's something I expect and I'm prepared for it.

The same thing applies to mental toxic waste. If I'm headed into a meeting with a co-worker who regularly loses his or her temper, I assume that the person's cork is going to pop at some point. If I get a voicemail from my cousin Jerry, who's always bugging me for money, I assume the conversation will turn toxic when I tell him I'm not giving him any.

Once I know where the waste is going to come from, I run through what I'm going to do if things go sideways. Sometimes I do that in my head, and sometimes I call someone on my team and rehearse the conversation. I'll have them throw me one curve ball after another, and I'll do my best to respond. We'll do this two or three or four times—whatever it takes for me to get comfortable if things hit the skids.

Make no mistake, though: The actual conversation never happens like I rehearse it, but that's not the point. Practicing the drill lets me bob and weave through the potentially toxic parts of an interaction so I come out on the other side without getting scorched.

2. Low-level toxic waste: Read the label.

You and I don't clean up nuclear waste or heavy metals that have leached out of a mining facility. But we do have experience handling low-level toxic waste: all the different products we use at home. When I thought about creating an action plan for myself on how to deal with mental low-level toxic waste, I figured the best thing to do was mimic a typical product label. That's what this whole book is about, right? Taking the knowledge and common sense from one area—emptying trash—and applying it to other areas, like cleaning out my mind. So, here goes: a warning label for managing low-level toxic waste.

DANGER!

Harmful if low-level toxic waste is continually swallowed. Contains irritants that can cause swelling of the ego, chafing of common sense, and scarring of long-term goals.

Do not mix with self-shredding thoughts, destructive behaviors, or unchallenged judgments from yourself or others. Keep out of reach of old patterns and behaviors that serve no purpose. Use with adequate mental ventilation.

Contents under pressure. Exposure to excess amounts of low-level toxic waste may cause sudden bursting and excess contamination of surrounding area. Keep from heat-of-the-moment decisions or open flame of act-now-and-regret-later.

TO PREVENT CONTAMINATION

Protect yourself. Keep eyes wide open when approaching potential sources of low-level toxic waste. Expect possibility of contamination; wear mental gloves and goggles to protect confidence and self-esteem.

Set boundaries. For example, decide how much backtalk to tolerate from kids when they're in a bad mood. Stop interacting with low-level toxic waste if boundary is crossed.

Say no. Decline toxic request or say no to a potentially noxious conversation. Reject obsessing over an issue. Do not give energy to deadbeat, one-way relationships.

Walk away. Stop conversation if voices are going up or words are getting nasty. Excuse yourself from the room or politely end the phone call. Re-engage only when cooled off and in control.

FIRST AID

Get away from source of contamination immediately.

Flush with mixture of "Is this TBO really true?" and "Is this how I want to spend my time and energy?"

If contamination is severe, call physician or mental health professional. Do not attempt to correct on your own!

3.   **High-level toxic waste: Suit up and get away.**

There's a four-step process the professionals use to deal with high-level toxic waste:

Prevention   Protection   Disposal   Restoration

This process also works great when high-level toxic waste shows up in my life. Here's how it breaks down.

Prevention is my attempt to avoid any direct contact between the hazard and myself. That may mean terminating a relationship, stopping a toxic conversation, or putting in for a transfer. Sometimes, it might involve legal action—a restraining order or a lawsuit—in order to keep the toxic waste away from me. The best thing I can do is avoid the contamination—or at a minimum, stop it from spreading.

If I have no choice but to be around the mess, then I move to the second step: *protection*. This is the mental equivalent of putting on my hazmat suit. I start with a basic threat assessment: What's vulnerable now that I'm in contact with toxic waste? Is it my family? A co-worker? My money? That tells me what immediate steps I have to take to protect what's valuable to me.

Then, I usually need some education to deal with what's in front of me. For example, if I find out that someone I care about has a drinking problem, I may need to read up on addiction or attend an AA meeting to learn more. I can't deal with serious situations if I don't know anything about what's going on. I need facts so I can make good decisions.

When it comes to *disposal* of the high-level toxic waste, I turn to the pros. You know what they say about the road to hell, that it's paved with good intentions? That is never truer than in the case of high-level toxic waste.

I cannot tell you the number of times I've taken on an issue that was way above my head only to screw it up even more. I once tried to help a friend with his gambling problem. Big mistake. Another time, I jumped into the middle of my cousin's custody dispute, thinking I could help everyone work things out. Once again, an epic failure. After a lot of bruises and cuts, I began to learn that there are some things I'm just not qualified to do. That doesn't mean I'm giving up or I don't care. Actually, it's the opposite. It means I have the good sense to step aside and let someone with the right skillset take over. That's going to improve the odds that the toxic mess can be contained and cleaned up.

Sometimes, I'm not completely sure whether the person or the situation I've run into is low- or high-level toxic waste—and that can affect how I respond to it. That's another thing the pros can help me with. Because they know their stuff, they can tell me what I'm facing, which means I'm not floundering, trying to figure out the right thing to do. They're also a great source for straight-up

WHEN PEOPLE OR SITUATIONS ARE TOXIC, THEY ARE USUALLY OUT OF CONTROL.

advice. Look, I know a lot about garbage, but I'm not an expert on human behavior. Getting tips from the pros can save me from making some really stupid mistakes.

I always have to remember that when people or situations are toxic, they are usually out of control. Innocent bystanders are getting run over. There's collateral damage. There's chaos and uncertainty. To stay safe, I remind myself that I'm not talking to the person I know. I'm talking to an alcoholic or a person who is suffering from an obsessive-compulsive disorder. If there are two of us in a room and the toxic person is unwilling or unable to be accountable for his or her actions, I try to be accountable for both of us. That's makes what I need to do pretty straightforward: Be on guard and stay connected to my action plan.

> I CAN MAKE A BAD SITUATION SO MUCH WORSE IF I TRY TO HANDLE A HIGH-LEVEL TOXIC SITUATION WITHOUT THE PROPER SKILLS.

At the end of the day, I can make a bad situation so much worse if I try to handle a high-level toxic situation without the proper skills. If it's a work-related problem, I'll bring it up to my supervisor or go talk to someone in HR. If it's outside of work, I'll contact a counselor or a lawyer or a specialist in alcohol intervention. These days, there's a specialist for just about everything, and these folks have very deep knowledge in their field. I have no hesitation in pulling them into a toxic situation, just like I'd never attempt to fix the transmission or the hydraulics on my truck. I'm going to take it to my mechanic who has way more experience repairing the big stuff than I ever will.

The last step is *restoration*. Once the high-level toxic waste has been removed, I need to assess the damage that's left behind. If I had to sever a relationship with someone in my group of friends, do I need to talk to everyone and clarify what happened? If I was nailed by identity theft, how do I restore my credit history? If I was the one who created a toxic mess at work or at home, do I need to make amends?

Sometimes, restoration means doing nothing at all. I once had my car stolen right out of my driveway. I called the police and my insurance company and sure enough, they found my car and arrested the thief. At his trial, the judge ordered him to pay me a thousand dollars of restitution. Do you think I went after him to collect? Once I found out he was a meth addict, had used my car to break into people's houses, and had prior convictions for illegal possession of guns, I wanted to stay as far away from him as possible. That was a case of leaving the damage as-is. I can live with it—especially when the restoration is too dangerous.

USE CAUTION

Whether it's low-level or high-level toxic waste, here are a few cautions that can mess up my ability to properly manage it.

WATCH OUT FOR INADVERTENT MIXING

Let's say I'm helping a friend deal with some low-level toxic waste. If I'm having toxic thoughts at the same time I'm helping him, his situation could easily contaminate us both, sucking me in as well as driving him deeper into the dumps.

If I'm going to purposely step into a low-level toxic situation, I need to make sure my head is in the right place first. What am I feeling? What's nagging at me? If I'm in a weird spot, it may not be the best time for me to be offering advice.

This can be challenging because people who are doling out low-level toxic waste don't necessarily realize that's what they're doing. Remember the chapter on ego? One of its characteristics is that we can't always tell when it's taken over the driver's seat. The same thing applies to toxic waste. Many of us can't sense our own level of toxicity. We're in so much pain or anguish that we don't feel the reality of where we are. That makes it easier to mix ourselves up in someone else's toxic waste.

BE RESPONSIBLE

Just because I see toxic waste doesn't make it my responsibility to clean it up. Sometimes, the best thing to do is offer a little advice on what's worked best for me, and let the other person decide what to do with it. When I step beyond that, I'm either resented for meddling or the other person expects me to do all the work. This ties back to the idea of boundaries. As long as I know where they are and I don't step beyond them, I can keep myself from getting tangled up in a big, toxic mess.

Speaking of acting responsibly, it's also up to me to manage my reaction to toxic waste when I run into it. Running around like a crazy man and throwing emotion off left and right isn't going to help the situation. Neither is tucking tail and running away. Toxic people and hazardous situations are part of life. The best defense against them is a level head and some forward planning.

SHOW RESPECT

Whether I'm the one generating the toxic waste or it's flowing from someone else, it's really important to show some respect for it. Having a plan is respectful. Charging in and acting as if I'm the one with all the answers is not.

I also need to respect anything that's toxic—or has the potential to be. Take wine, for example. Having a glass with dinner has been done for thousands of years. So has using it to get drunk. That's the line I walk with things in my life that are toxic. What can seem harmless can turn deadly if I'm not careful. I'm not suggesting that you should be afraid of wine or run away from it, only

> I ALSO NEED TO RESPECT ANYTHING THAT'S TOXIC—OR HAS THE POTENTIAL TO BE.

that it deserves respect because of its ability to turn hazardous and create some real and lasting havoc.

REMEMBER THE CONSEQUENCES

At our morning briefing a few months back, I heard about garbage service that was suspended in a neighborhood. It turns out that a bunch of folks had been using a vacant lot down the street to work on their cars. They had been doing it for years and over time, oil, gas, paint thinner, and other chemicals had seeped into the ground. The authorities found out, and tests revealed that the entire lot was thoroughly contaminated. Plus, the mess was leaching into a small creek nearby, sending pollution miles downstream. Needless to say, it was going to take a lot of time and money to clean it all up.

That taught me an important lesson: there are always consequences to what I do, and they add up over time. Whenever the words "That's not a big deal" cross my mind, I stop and ask myself, "Really?" There have been some great books written on the compounding effect small consequences can have over many years. The result often times leads to toxic situations like obesity, bankruptcy, and divorce. However, the more I remember that there are consequences to my actions, the more I can prevent them from ever turning toxic.

TAKING IT TO THE STREET

SUMMARY: GET AWAY FROM TOXIC WASTE

Toxic waste is a type of garbage that's in a class of its own and that needs special care and handling. It can't just be tossed into my personal landfill or treated like a normal TBO. It's a real threat to my route, my goals, and potentially my health if I'm not careful.

There are two types of mental toxic waste: low-level and high-level. Low-level toxic TBOs are like household chemicals with warning labels: okay in small doses, dangerous if abused. High-level toxic TBOs are the really bad stuff—abusive relationships or drug abuse—and usually need a professional to help contain and clean up. Sometimes, I walk headfirst into a toxic situation; other times, it gradually turns toxic on its own. Wherever it comes from though, I have to know how to handle it before it has a chance to do any damage.

Living a toxic-free life has a lot of benefits. I can stop playing the victim, stop contaminating myself and others, and kick fear of certain situations right to the curb. Isolating toxic relationships and hazardous thoughts is a great way to take my power back. Harmful, nasty TBOs don't control me anymore. I do.

Managing low-level toxic waste uses a lot of the same rules as using Drano or bleach: Don't mix TBOs, protect myself, and use common sense. Dealing with high-level toxic waste means donning a hazmat suit and calling in professionals to help with the situation—always a good idea when I don't have the skills to fix what's in front of me.

EXERCISES

1. **Find one example of low-level toxic waste and one example of high-level toxic waste in your life. (If you can't find a current example, use something from your past.) Describe the effect that this toxic waste is having on you.**

---

2. **For the low-level toxic waste example: Write your own warning label, using the guide below.**

   - Danger! (What are the dangers to you if you don't handle this low-level toxic waste correctly?)

   - To Prevent Contamination (What would you need to do in order to avoid contaminating yourself?)

   - First Aid (If you come into contact with the low-level toxic waste, what steps would you take to contain the damage and fix what went wrong?)

   _____

   _____

   _____

   _____

   _____

   _____

   _____

   _____

   _____

3. **For the high-level toxic waste example:**

    ▪ Perform a threat assessment. Who is in danger of being contaminated by this waste?

    ▪ What do you need to do in order to educate yourself about the problem? Be specific here, listing what areas you don't know about and what resources you might investigate to learn more.

    ▪ What professionals would be needed to contain this situation? How would you approach them for help?

    _____

    _____

    _____

    _____

    _____

    _____

    _____

    _____

    _____

STEP 7
STOP HOARDING

*"The mountains of things we throw away are much greater than the things we use.
In this, if in no other way, we can see the wild and reckless exuberance of our production,
and waste seems to be the index."*
—*John Steinbeck*

I took my wife and kids to the circus a few weeks ago. The time came for the trapeze artist to do his act. He leaped off the platform, grabbed the bar, and swung forward. A few seconds later, his momentum ran out and he swung back toward the platform. After five or six times, I realized that until he let go of the bar to grab the next one in front of him, those were his only two choices: go forward until he ran out of gas or go back to where he started.

Finally, he did it: He let go of the bar. Everything went quiet as he flew through empty air. This was the moment of risk, that no-man's land where it was too late for him to turn back but no guarantee of where he was going to end up.

Then, he found the second trapeze and swung all the way to the other side of the arena. I figured the first few times he did that, it had to be pretty scary. But with some practice and the belief that he'd make it to the other side, he had obviously overcome that fear. And now, it's probably second nature to him.

Do you remember the garage I talked about a couple of chapters ago—the one that used to be crammed full of stuff until we finally cleaned it out? If I think about it, it's exactly the same as that trapeze guy.

The garage was a mess because we couldn't let go of all the stuff in there. We thought we'd need it. We felt attached to it. We assumed the kids would want it. We thought we were in control of it. But we were totally wrong. It was in control of us. All we could do is swing back and forth in the limited area that we had there.

It was only when we realized that the garage was actually full of useless junk from our past that we were finally able to let it all go. And that moved us further along, just like the trapeze artist. We have a place to park our cars inside. We can find what we need. And we're not hoarding junk in there anymore. Was it scary when we were giving everything up? Absolutely! Did we have second thoughts as we were hauling everything away? You bet we did! But in the end, the reward was totally worth the risk.

Look, I know how to empty garbage. I do it at home and I do it for a living. But I learned from watching that guy flying through the air that some garbage is harder to throw out than other garbage if you don't first learn to let go. And that's what I want to talk about in this chapter: why I hoard mental garbage in my head just like we hoarded physical garbage in our garage. Because once I got a handle on that, I was able to throw out all the trash and keep my life moving in the direction I wanted. So here goes: my take on hoarding. Because together, we can leave the old trash behind—for good.

WHAT IS HOARDING?

If I take a look at all the garbage that I create in my head, I'm able to toss most of it if I really make an effort. However, depending on where I am in my life, I always notice that some TBOs are really hard to throw away. Even though I've learned a ton about dumping mental trash, I still keep around certain thoughts, beliefs, and opinions that are anchored in my past and that knock me off my route. That's what I call hoarding: hanging on to mental garbage that I know I should throw out.

Remember the concept of segments—dividing your life up into specific areas like Love, Career, and Marriage? When I hoard, I'm usually holding on to negative TBOs in a specific segment. Sometimes, it's just one segment: *I'm a crummy parent*. Other times, I'll create a little hoarding collection across multiple segments: obsessing about my job, the way I handle money, and what I think about my weight—even if I'm regularly tossing mental trash in all my other segments. Also, what I hoard changes because I'm not the same guy I was a day or a year or a decade ago. Life keeps coming at me, which

What inner garbage are you hoarding? Why is it hard for you to let it go?

means I'm always making new garbage up around what happens. Some of it I can dump and some of it I hoard. So yeah, hoarding can be a moving target.

Ever get a coupon for something that's on sale for 70 percent off the regular price? All of a sudden, the value of that item goes up. If it's that much of a deal, it's worth a look, right? My brain gets so plugged in to what's in front of it that I don't stop and ask myself, "Do I really need that?" That's what hoarding does: It psyches me into thinking that certain TBOs have a lot of value and makes me want to keep them, when in fact they have no value at all.

Hoarding has two sides to it. The first is *getting*. Just like people who can't stop buying things they don't need, when I get an idea like *I'm overweight* in my head, I can't stop piling on the negative TBOs that are related to it: *My stomach is too big, I'm really looking old,* and so on. Pretty soon, it gets so bad that I can't walk by a mirror without my brain generating some nasty thought about how bad I look. It's like a mega-magnet that attracts every negative TBO I can create.

The second part of hoarding is the *getting rid of*. If I were collecting a zillion TBOs about my weight, but dumping them really quickly into my landfill, I wouldn't be hoarding. I'd be emptying my mental trash. However, if I keep bringing the TBOs in, and I can't or won't let them go, I'm hoarding.

Hoarding is the opposite of emptiness. Emptiness is created when I throw out mental trash. Hoarding takes place when I keep clinging to mental trash in a specific segment. If I'm hoarding, I can't create emptiness, and without emptiness, there's no opportunity, no vision, and no possibility to expand my thinking. If I feel stuck in a segment, one of the first things I'll do is see if I'm hoarding negative TBOs. If I am, I know it's time to do some targeted mental housecleaning.

WHAT I HOARD

I used to think of hoarding purely in physical terms: rooms crammed full of newspapers and boxes piled one on top of the other. But that's just what you can see. When it comes to mental hoarding, there are all kinds of different things my brain will cling to and won't let go. Here are a few of them, along with the clues that tell me my mind is probably hoarding.

Unhelpful TBOs about time. Sometimes, I'll start hoarding thoughts about being short on time by creating a hundred variations of *There just aren't enough hours in the day.* And before I know it, I've convinced myself that I'll never finish a project or accomplish a goal—and I'll give up before I even start.

Negative TBOs about information. There's so much information out there that I make up a ton of TBOs about it: *I'll get left behind* *if I don't read it all* and *I'm an idiot because my nine-year-old knows more about computers than I do.* It doesn't take long before I overcompensate by saving everything and convincing myself that I'll circle back and read it all later (which of course, I never have the time to do). I have so many bookmarks in my browser menu that they scroll off the screen. There are so many files on my computer desktop that I can't even see the background and I have hundreds of old emails in my inbox that I've read but never deleted. Here's the real irony: When I can't find a file or a website in that mess, I blame the computer instead of the real culprit—my need to digitally hoard everything!

Drama. If I'm in a funk, I'll start picking fights or overreacting to situations, creating a pile of unnecessary drama and conflict. Then, I'll hoard that drama and use it as justification for what I'm doing: "Well, Fred always flies off the handle, so why can't I?"

TBOs that make me a victim. I'm really good at this one: telling the whole world, "Look at me—a guy who always comes in last" when I'm feeling sorry for myself. Maybe I got the short end of the stick or I tried something and failed. No matter what happened, I hoard victim TBOs that let everyone know I fell on my face.

Disappointments. When things don't work the way I'd planned or hoped, I hoard as a way of dealing with my disappointment. For example, I hold on to thoughts like *I can't stand my boss* and *This is a dead-end job* when I don't get a promotion I was expecting.

What I hoard changes depending on what's going on in my life. If I've hit a rough patch at home, I'll hoard negative TBOs about how tough it is to be married. If I'm facing health issues, I'll hoard beliefs about how badly I take care of myself. Hoarding doesn't necessarily mean I've been piling things up for a long time. Sometimes, it only takes a day or two for me to create a big pile of TBOs if something in my

> WHAT I HOARD CHANGES DEPENDING ON WHAT'S GOING ON IN MY LIFE.

life goes sideways. And that pile can become a real issue if I don't get it under control.

If I really listen to the thoughts that are running through my brain, it's pretty easy to see the places where I'm thinking about the same thing over and over again. That's what I'm hoarding: the negative TBOs I don't want to let go and that keep my segments filled with clutter and chaos. I also deny myself the Empty Zones I need to expand and grow in that area—which makes me feel stuck in the same place. That can be very frustrating, especially if other parts of my life feel like they have some momentum. And I'll tell you something else: The energy I chew up holding on to those problems would be a whole lot better spent finding solutions for them instead. What does hoarding get me, anyway? Nothing but resentment, anxiety, and stress—none of which will help me get out of the dumps.

WHY I HOARD

Now that I've defined what hoarding is, the next question is why I do it in the first place.

Fear. This is probably the biggest reason why I hoard TBOs. Tossing thoughts and opinions I've held on to for a zillion years feels like I'm getting rid of a part of myself—and that's pretty scary, especially when I don't have anything to replace it. Like that trapeze artist I talked about earlier, there's no guarantee where I'll end up once I let go. Will I be happy? Will I land on my feet? There's no way to know, and that can be really scary. So my mind grabs on to whatever will

What are the major reasons why you hoard your mental garbage? Do you usually hoard in one specific area?

make that fear go away and hoards it like crazy. So for that part of my life, I'm stuck until I let the fear go.

Not liking where I am. Life can be brutal sometimes. I'm cruising down the road, minding my own business, when I hit a rough patch with my wife and we're arguing all the time. At that moment, living in the here and now doesn't feel so great, so I'll look over my shoulder and reminisce about my bachelor days. Things were so much simpler back then! No responsibilities. Only myself to worry about. No hassles with women. Before I know it, I've created and hoarded a slew of negative TBOs about my current life. *Being married is really hard. I'm a lousy husband. She'd be better off without me.* I pile them on, one after another, until I've convinced myself that marriage is a big bummer.

Never mind that the guy in his twenties was doing the exact same thing: hoarding idealized TBOs about how much easier life was when I was a teenager. And forget about the fact that I always romanticize my past and conveniently forget about all the problems I used to have. Pining for my past gives me an easy out from dealing with why things are lousy right now. I'm not saying that reminiscing is a bad thing. It's an important part of life, but it can't be my whole life. And if I'm not careful, it can lead to hoarding a bunch of negative TBOs that can shut down one of my segments.

Control. If a segment is causing me problems, hoarding a pile of TBOs makes me feel like I have some control over it. If I'm obsessing, I must be solving, right? Here's the truth. I usually get much better results when I throw out the TBOs I'm hoarding and create some emptiness in that segment. Nine times out of ten, that gives me the mental breathing room I need to see things from a different perspective and create some new, positive TBOs that get me where I need to be. That's when I feel I'm really in control of the problem—and I can find my own solution.

Trauma. There is no doubt that the big events—deaths of those close to us, a serious financial loss, or a major injury—take their toll. I had a scare with a heart attack a few years ago, and whenever

I run into a health issue, the first place I go is back to that event. I start hoarding negative TBOs left and right: *I'm dying again, I can't be healthy no matter what I do, my body is broken,* and on and on.

There are other reasons why my mind hoards unhealthy TBOs, including family issues, stubbornness, force of habit, and old patterns I learned as a kid (my mom was a big hoarder). Whatever the reason, I've learned that saving TBOs because I might use them someday is like filling my garage with piles of junk. That "someday" rarely arrives and the chances that I'll ever get value out of reusing an old TBO is usually slim to none. That means instead of the emptiness I need so badly, I'm getting nothing but the clutter of old garbage that really needs to be thrown out.

THE SYMPTOMS OF HOARDING

Once I started watching my own behavior, I began to see certain symptoms that gave me a clue that I was hoarding. That was a big first step toward stopping the habit and throwing out this excess trash. So here's a list of my most common symptoms. See if any of these fit for you.

Chaos. I've seen pictures of hoarders' offices and houses. It's pure chaos inside: bags, clothes, piles of paper, a microwave oven sitting on the dining room table. That is exactly what my head feels like when I'm hoarding TBOs. I'm scatterbrained and disorganized. It's hard to concentrate because my mind keeps thinking about the same TBO over and over again.

When I was little, I used to love going to my grandfather's office. He had a big wooden desk that was completely covered with papers, so many that they made an arc about a foot and a half tall. The phone would ring and he'd thrust his hand into that pile and dig around until he found what he was looking for. Sure, that monster pile had some sort of organization to it, but no matter how you slice it, his desk was pure chaos.

Defensiveness. When I'm hoarding, I get really defensive, especially when my TBOs are challenged. I'll get all self-righteous—"Hey, I have every right to feel this way!"—and I'll find myself justifying whatever it is I'm hoarding. When I notice myself mentally digging in, that's a big clue that I'm at it again.

> WHEN I NOTICE MYSELF MENTALLY DIGGING IN, THAT'S A BIG CLUE THAT I'M HOARDING.

That goes hand in hand with resistance to change. People who hoard generally resist change, and I'm no exception to that. Change means risk and uncertainty and sometimes, I don't want to deal with that. That's why I won't let a TBO go once I've sunk my teeth into it. When the word "no" keeps coming out of my mouth on a regular basis, there's a good chance I'm hoarding something.

Shutting out. Some people hoard in specific places in their house—the garage or a bedroom—and they won't let anyone near that space. When I'm going through a mental hoarding episode, I do exactly the same thing: shut people out of certain areas of my life. I'll dodge conversations or change the subject to distract them. My wife loves to call me out on this one, and she's almost always right. When I clam up, it's usually because I'm hoarding something.

Changing the intended purpose. If you look inside a chronic hoarder's house, you can't use the tub to take a bath or the couch to sit down because they're full of junk. That's a major symptom of hoarding: things can't be used for their intended purpose anymore.

Mental hoarding works the same way. A negative TBO like *Love isn't worth the effort* might have gotten me through a heart-wrenching breakup twenty years ago, but what about now? If it's driving a wedge between my wife and me or blocking my ability to bond with my kids, that's a million miles away from its original intended purpose.

I have other symptoms of mental hoarding: putting off important decisions, anxiety,
or looking at mental housecleaning as a major task. All of these mean the same thing:
I've stashed away certain TBOs and my
mind doesn't want to let them go. Good-bye
emptiness. Hello clutter and chaos.

> I'VE STASHED AWAY
> CERTAIN TBOs AND MY
> MIND DOESN'T WANT
> TO LET THEM GO.

I had a friend years ago who told me that when he first got
out of college, he was a total workaholic. Eighty- and ninety-hour
workweeks were normal, and he practically lived at his desk. One
day, he picked up the new edition of the employee magazine (he
worked at a big company) and saw a photo of a buddy who worked
in another department. The two of them had been hired at the same
time and they had a running competition to see who would be promoted first. My friend said he was grinning from ear to ear when
he saw the photo—until he opened the magazine.

The friend had died in a plane crash.

He remembered the news stories about an airliner that had
gone down shortly after takeoff. More than a hundred fifty dead.
He knew his buddy had regularly flown in and out of that airport
but he had been so busy with work that he had hardly paid attention. He completely missed the fact that a good friend, a colleague
at his own company, had died. He realized that he was hoarding a
huge pile of negative TBOs about his career: Everyone was going to
pass him up, and if he didn't work hard enough, he'd be fired. His
fear-based TBOs about his performance had caused him to let his
job completely fill up his life. In an instant, he realized how much it
was costing him and how out of balance he was.

That's when he started making changes. He cut back on his
working hours. He started dating. He spent time with his family
and friends. He still had a really successful career, but he told me it

was in proportion with everything else. Ever since he told me that story, I always remember it whenever hoarding threatens to take over a part of my life, because the last thing I want is to lose touch with what's really important.

WHEN DOES HOLDING BECOME HOARDING?

Every Wednesday, the local newspaper company delivers a free supplement filled with recipes and a ton of ads from all the supermarkets. Sometimes, I'm just too lazy to go and pick it up, so it just sits there at the end of my driveway. By Saturday or Sunday, I stop noticing it. It's like the paper has become part of the concrete and I just don't see it anymore. That raises an interesting point: When I stop noticing my mental garbage, I'm probably in the crosshairs for hoarding.

A belief like *I need to be cautious around people until I know they're trustworthy* is a good rule to live by, so I'm going to keep it around. The problem is when I stop realizing that it's in my head, just like that newspaper in the driveway. That's when a helpful TBO can easily morph over time into something bad. *Be cautious* turns into *Don't trust anyone.* That becomes the new standard that I judge people by and, pretty soon, I'm hoarding all sorts of related TBOs. Holding becomes hoarding when I let my attention lapse and take my eyes off the kinds of thoughts I have in my mind.

> HOLDING BECOMES HOARDING WHEN I LET MY ATTENTION LAPSE.

Don't get me wrong. Collecting and holding is not a bad thing. I store extra food in the pantry and I store important papers in the file cabinet. I also hold on to good TBOs that keep offering me guidance and direction. It's an instinct and a critical part of survival: holding on to things that I'm going to need later. However, there's a big difference between storing and hoarding. One is a necessity;

the other is an obsession. It's a question of moderation, of knowing where to draw the line between hanging on to healthy TBOs and hoarding the unhealthy ones that keep dragging me down.

STOP DRAGGING IT FORWARD

Let's say I go on a trip and I stop in a bunch of small towns. I pick up a few souvenirs in the first place and shove them into the small suitcase I'm carrying with me. I do the same in the second town, and the third, not even thinking about what I bought before. All I care about is what's in front of me, right now—and I want it. Pretty soon, the pile of stuff I'm dragging from town to town is getting bigger and heavier. Does that stop me when I see another souvenir shop? Are you kidding? Out comes the wallet again...

This is exactly what I do with the unhealthy TBOs that I've hoarded: drag them from one stage of my life to the next, no matter how big and heavy that pile may be. Those TBOs may be old and outdated, but it doesn't matter. If I'm hoarding them, I'll force-fit those old beliefs into the life I'm leading now. What would happen if I stopped doing that? What would life look like?

First, I'd open up lots of new space in my head. I'd have valuable emptiness that gives me the breathing room I need to think clearly. Instead of being preoccupied with all the TBOs I'm hoarding, I get to spend time thinking about new things that carry me in the direction I really want to go.

Second, my brain is going to be a lot lighter now that I've cleared out all the hoarded TBOs that I keep stuffing in there. Instead of hauling that garbage around and having it knock me sideways all the time, it's gone, which means I don't have that constant, irritating voice in the back of my head droning on about the same thing over and over again.

When I stop hoarding, I get to kick fear to the curb. Instead of TBOs telling me that change is scary and terrible, I get to see it in an entirely new light: a challenge, an opportunity to try something new, a chance to stretch myself in a new direction. Will I still be nervous when things start to change? Will there be a few stabs of "uh-oh"? Of course. I'm human! But those feelings don't rule me anymore once I stop hoarding. They don't stop me from going for what I really want.

I've also noticed that when I stop hoarding, I get less drama. I think it's related to the chaos factor I talked about earlier. The more I pile up negative TBOs in this area or that, the more chaotic my life feels. And when I'm swimming in chaos, I'm usually on edge, reacting first instead of thinking things through. That's all I need to create a big pile of drama and drive everyone around me nuts. When I stop hoarding, all of that calms down. I'm more even-keeled and level. No one runs for cover when I walk into the room. When I'm not obsessing about my weight or my marriage or the fact that my hairline is receding, I'm quieter inside. Why? I have access to my emptiness, which means I have room to do the job of the garbageman: throw out the mental trash I don't need, including TBOs that I'm hoarding.

LETTING PEOPLE BACK IN

Hoarders don't want people to see the mess inside their homes, either because they're embarrassed or they don't want their collection to be disturbed. All that junk is like the moat around a castle. It's protection that they think they can't do without, a barrier to keep them safe.

When I stop hoarding thoughts, I'm taking down that barrier. I let people back in to places in my life. I'm not saying that I want to skip down the street and sing "Kumbaya" all day long. It's more like taking a deep breath, putting my hand on the knob, and slowly opening the door. For a guy who's pretty good at keeping his distance, putting the brakes on my hoarding habit is a great way to free up some valuable real estate in my head—space that can be used to let both people and new ideas back in again.

PUTTING MY TOYS AWAY

The more I work this idea of tossing my mental trash, the more ways I find why it doesn't make sense for me to hoard old garbage.

Back when I was a kid, life came at me left and right. Almost everything was a new experience: getting picked on, having a favorite aunt die, really liking a girl. My little brain didn't have a clue how to deal with all of this input, so it made up TBOs along the way to help it cope.

Now, flash forward and here I am, a fully grown man. I have adult responsibilities now: a job, a wife, and a couple of kids. If I don't get rid of my mental trash, which is made up of decades-old TBOs, I'll be making important, potentially life-changing decisions using thoughts, beliefs, and opinions I made up about myself *when I was a kid!* That makes no sense at all! Those ancient TBOs are completely out of sync with who I am today.

> ANCIENT TBOs ARE COMPLETELY OUT OF SYNC WITH WHO I AM TODAY.

Listen, I eventually outgrew my tricycle, my baseball cards, and the crush I had on my seventh-grade science teacher. So you'd think that I would also outgrow all my old TBOs, right? Well, my brain doesn't work like that. I don't automatically outgrow my mental trash. I have to make the decision to throw it away. Unfortunately, no one taught me that I was supposed to do that, so here I am, a grown man still being run by the opinions of a twelve-year-old.

Putting away my childish ideas of life does more for me than just end hoarding. It also gives me more control over my emotions. Think about it. If most of my childhood TBOs are based on feelings, not intellect, throwing those out means I'm also getting rid of a lot of emotional baggage. That frees my mind to use rational thought and all my street smarts to solve problems—and that usually means getting out of the dumps faster and staying on the route I created for myself. And that makes me happy.

HOARDING SCHOOL

Since no one taught me about hoarding when I was little, I figured it was time to create Hoarding School: a way to stop hanging on to thoughts, beliefs, and opinions that are getting me nowhere. I have a lot I want to accomplish in life—and I can't do it if I'm holding on to piles of unhelpful TBOs that do nothing but clutter up my route.

1. Figure out what I'm hoarding—and why.

An outsider will often look at a hoarder's home or apartment and think that all they have to do is clean out the junk and everything will be fine. Unfortunately, it's not that easy.

Hoarding isn't about emptying trash. I can't just dump it and say, "There. I'm no longer hoarding." The root causes for mental hoarding run deeper than that. To really stop it, I first have to figure out which TBOs I'm hoarding and the reasons why I'm so determined to hang on to them.

Let's start with the first part. To figure out what I'm hoarding, I need to pay attention to the stream of thoughts floating through my head. I have to admit to myself that I'm holding on to trash and that I'm putting myself through my own misery. That kind of honesty can be tough, especially if I don't want to face certain issues in my life. But I can't hide from what I'm hoarding if I want to stop it. I have to look it in the eye and admit that I have a problem with it.

> I CAN'T HIDE FROM WHAT I'M HOARDING IF I WANT TO STOP IT.

Once I've done that, I use a couple of techniques to help me figure out why I won't let the TBOs go.

- I'll ask myself how long I've been holding on to the TBO. Is it recent? Am I reacting to something going on around me (for example, I'm hoarding all kinds of *I'm terrible with money* TBOs because I'm short on cash)? Or is this a TBO that I've had for a long time (for example, believing for ten years that no one really thinks I'm smart)? Sometimes, the length of time I've kept a TBO will help me figure out the reason I'm so attached to it.

- I'll focus on what my hoarding is costing me in order to cut its value. Physical hoarders are told to add up how much they've spent on acquiring new possessions in the past year or calculate the value of the junk they're hoarding. This also applies to mental hoarding. I ask questions like these: What's the purpose of this unhelpful TBO that I'm hoarding? What payoff am I getting from hoarding it (for example, do I always get sympathy or does it help me get my way)? The goal is to put my hoarding in a cold, objective light. Nine times out of ten, this helps me see that the cost of the TBO is way higher than any benefit I'm getting.

2. Isolate the junk.

Once hoarders begin the actual process of throwing out their junk, they're told to put things into piles: what they use regularly (at least once a week), what they use occasionally (once every six months), and what they hardly use at all. This technique works great with garbage TBOs that I'm mentally hoarding.

Once I figure out the specific TBOs that I'm holding on to, I ask myself if I'm using it and, if so, how often. Unlike physical hoarders who are taught just to toss things they hardly use at all, a hoarded TBO can be a real pain, whether I use it every day or once a decade.

Here's a great example of that. I had to give a safety talk in front of all the other drivers. I wrote down what I wanted to say, practiced, and timed myself so I wouldn't drone on. While I was preparing though, there was this voice running through the back of my mind: "You're a terrible public speaker and you're going to screw this up." I didn't notice it at first, but once I became aware of it, I started asking myself why I was thinking like that.

Then it hit me. When I was in sixth grade, I ran for student body president. I had to stand up in front of the entire school and make a speech. To be clever, I wrote a speech that assigned each letter of my first name to a word that said why I'd make a great leader. When I stepped up to the microphone though, I was so nervous that I couldn't get past the first letter. You should have heard me:

"The S stands for stupor."

Roaring laughter.

"The S stands for scooper."

Even more laughter.

Then, someone shouted out, "Move on to the next letter!"

I felt like I had just fallen out of the stupid tree and hit every branch on the way down. I was mortified by what happened! Right then and there, I made up a nasty TBO that I was a terrible public speaker. That little gem sat in the corner of my head for decades. Sure, I eventually forgot about it, but the experience left such a strong mark on me, that TBO wasn't going anywhere.

Now, fast forward to my safety talk—my first public speaking gig since sixth grade. Guess what shows up? That's right: a forty-year-old belief that I suck in front of a crowd. And in a matter of days, I'm hoarding a pile of other TBOs just like it: *No one will like what I have to say. Everyone will notice that I've put on some weight. My voice sounds weird.* A fully grown man still haunted by a silly TBO

I made up when I was a kid. Boy, was I glad to finally isolate that one.

3. Let it go.

Once I've isolated what I'm hoarding, it's time to let it go. That means tossing it into my personal landfill just like I do with my other mental trash. Even though it's regular garbage and I can get rid of it like any other TBO, I have to remember that it may feel harder to toss it, like I'm giving up a part of my personality.

When I was younger, I used to brag about not needing to exercise. I was skinny, my gut was flat, and I could eat what I wanted and never gain a pound. Then, I hit my forties and my body started to change—and not for the better. I knew the time had come to start taking better care of myself. Yet, giving up that *I don't need exercise* mentality was really hard. It had been part of how I thought for so long, tossing those TBOs felt really difficult.

If I find that I'm having trouble throwing out hoarded TBOs, I ask myself a simple question: "What's the worst that will happen to me if I let this go?" Thinking like that lets me drag any fears I have out into the open, where I can then ask myself how real they are and how likely they'll come true. What I usually discover is that they're worst-case and overblown, and things hardly *ever* turn out as bad as I imagine.

> THE BEST THING TO DO WITH HOARDED TRASH IS TO LET IT GO. THAT REALLY HELPS ME PUT IT INTO MY LANDFILL SO I CAN MOVE ON.

So, the best thing I can do with hoarded trash is to let it go. I remind myself that it's not toxic. It's just regular garbage that I've become especially attached to and if I can toss mental trash in all the other areas of my life, I can get rid of hoarded trash, too. That really helps me put it into my landfill so I can move on and create those all-important Empty Zones I need to clear my head and refocus on my goals.

4. Get help.

Hoarders often use professionals to help them bring their condition under control. Counseling, medication, and behavior modification are great tools to help chronic hoarders stare down their issues and take their lives back again.

If I'm having trouble getting on top of my mental hoarding, I don't think twice about adding a professional to my team. These folks have a ton of experience helping people manage their hoarding issues and are the perfect way to help me get rid of TBOs that I can't seem to shake. And if I think there's any stigma associated with bringing a pro into the mix, forget about it. As I've said all along, finding the right person for the job isn't just practical. It's smart.

USE CAUTION

Here are a few things that can affect my efforts to stop hoarding.

Start Slow

When hoarders reach out for help to start cleaning up, one of the first pieces of advice they get is to start slow. It's pretty intimidating to stare at a huge pile of accumulated junk. Where do you begin? What do you toss first? Well, like any big project, they're told not to try to do it all at once. Start with a drawer. Then, move on to a closet. Then, tackle a bedroom.

That's really great advice for mental hoarding. When I find TBOs that I don't want to let go, I don't try to dump them all at once. I use the Hoarding School techniques to chip away at them. After all, it took me months and years to hoard them. It's unrealistic to expect that I'm going to suddenly toss them all in one fell swoop—especially if the reason I'm hoarding them is rooted in some deep, serious stuff. Slow and steady wins this race. Eventually, I'll shake them off.

WATCH OUT FOR THE GOOD STUFF

In this chapter, I've talked about hoarding the bad stuff: negative TBOs that I use to beat up a certain aspect of myself. Well, there's a flip side to hoarding that's equally as bad—and easy to miss if I'm not careful.

Let's say I'm going through a rough stage in my career. For some reason, I'm not feeling good about being a garbageman, so I'm hoarding all kinds of negative TBOs—thoughts like *I'll never get promoted* and *The younger guys are way better than I am*. So I use the Hoarding School directives to help me stop. If I'm not careful, I can slowly start to hoard the new TBOs that helped me get rid of the old one—thoughts like *I'm so good at dumping trash that I'll be the next one promoted* or *I'm way better than the new guys*. If I keep that up for too long, I'm going to cross the line into arrogance and bragging.

When I look at what I'm hoarding, I don't just look for negative TBOs. I have to make sure I'm not hoarding excess positive thoughts that can also skew the way I think and act. I'm not saying that I shouldn't believe in myself. It's like everything else related to hoarding: Keep it balanced and keep it in perspective.

TOSSING VS. REARRANGING

I have to laugh. My route supervisor is a paper hoarder. He has stacks of file folders all over his office that he never puts away. Whenever I go in to see him, it's always the same routine. He takes all the folders off his desk, puts them on the floor, and says, "There. Much better. What can I do for you?"

He didn't clean his desk by tossing what he was hoarding. He just rearranged it.

I'm an expert at using rationalization, excuses, and justifications to move the garbage around in my mind. Doing that may make me feel better, but I never really get rid of it. Rearranging is not the same as emptying, and it doesn't put a stop to hoarding. So if

REARRANGING IS NOT THE SAME AS EMPTYING.

that's my goal, moving the piles around is not the answer. Getting rid of them is.

TAKING IT TO THE STREET

SUMMARY: STOP HOARDING

Sometimes, trash can be very hard for me to toss. If I'm unhappy in a certain area of my life—let's say I'm having a hassle with my boss—I start hoarding unhealthy TBOs like *I must be hard to get along with* or *This job sucks.* One TBO starts attracting another until I have this pile of garbage that I find really hard to let go.

I hoard in different areas: communication, time, drama, or victim. I hoard because I'm afraid of what's going to happen in the future or because I'm having a problem at home or at work. When my world feels chaotic, I'm shutting people out, and I'm defensive and snapping at everybody, there's a pretty good chance I'm hoarding.

When I stop, life always looks better. I don't drag twenty- and thirty-year-old TBOs everywhere I go. I put away some of the childish beliefs that I don't need anymore and replace them with more rational, grown-up TBOs. Stopping my hoarding habit is like getting a software upgrade for my brain. Everything runs better and I get a much more up-to-date set of programming instructions!

WHEN MY OBSESSION FOR A PART OF MY PAST STARTS BLOCKING MY FUTURE, THAT'S HOARDING.

There's nothing wrong with understanding my past and examining the TBOs that I hold on to. It's what this book is all about. I *have* to know where I came from and what makes me tick in order to create a route to my future. At the same time, when my obsession for a part of my past starts blocking my future, that's hoarding—and I need to take steps to end it.

EXERCISES

1. Find an area in your life where you're hoarding a specific thought, belief, or opinion—even if you're regularly throwing out trash everywhere else.

_____

_____

_____

_____

_____

2. Write down why you think you are hoarding it.

_____

_____

_____

_____

_____

3. What symptoms show up when you're hoarding this particular TBO?

_____

_____

_____

_____

_____

4. How long have you been hoarding this TBO?

    _____

    _____

    _____

    _____

    _____

5. In one column, make a list of the value you receive from
    hoarding this TBO. On the other side, make a list of what you
    think it's costing you to hold on to it.

    _____   _____

    _____   _____

    _____   _____

    _____   _____

    _____   _____

6. How often do you use this hoarded TBO?

    _____

    _____

    _____

    _____

    _____

7. Can you let the hoarded TBO go? If not, what are your worst
    fears about letting it go? How likely is it that these worst-case
    scenarios will happen?

    _____

    _____

    _____

    _____

    _____

STEP 8
TAKE CARE OF YOUR TRUCK

"Nothing prevents maintenance like preventative maintenance."
—Keith Elder

When I pull into the yard at the end of the day, there's always a line of trucks waiting for the maintenance shop. What gets me is that they're usually the same trucks driven by the same guys. Because those vehicles aren't on the road, and because we have to finish every route every day, it sometimes lands on me to make up the slack and cover the work they didn't get done. This screws up the daily schedule, costs the company extra money, and stresses out our customers when we're late.

I'm not saying that my truck is perfect and never needs service. My brakes wear out, the oil needs changing, and every few years it might need a new paint job. However, I don't find myself in that maintenance line very often because I know that without my truck, I can't do my job. So I take good care of that vehicle by driving it carefully and making sure it gets maintained.

Throughout this book, I've talked about how important it is to dump my mental trash. I've given examples of how to find it and how to get rid of it. However, none of that can happen if I don't take care of my personal truck—otherwise known as my body.

You see, my body and my truck are identical in a lot of ways. They both are a network of mechanical, electrical, and chemical systems all working together. As sophisticated as they are though, these machines have a lot of moving parts that need maintenance and support to stay in good running condition.

Haulers spend hundreds of thousands of dollars on their vehicles. It's an investment they have to make if they want their businesses to grow and thrive. I'm doing the same thing: investing in my family, my career, and in myself. That raises a simple question: How am I going to take care of that investment?

Just like there's a direct relationship between a truck and how it's driven, I've learned that there's a direct relationship between my mind and my body. When I mistreat my body by overeating or getting drunk or not going to the doctor, it's hard to keep my mind in order. The opposite is true, too. Letting my mind go to the dogs and filling it up with a bunch of garbage is going to affect how I treat my body. It's hard to create Empty Zones and start thinking in new and creative directions if I'm exhausted and worn out. If I want proof of that, I only need to think about what I do to myself when I'm down in the dumps.

That's why it makes sense that the last step to emptying mental trash is taking care of my truck. When my body isn't working properly, the garbage isn't moving. With so much that I want to accomplish in my life, I don't want the burden of all that trash anymore. The more I keep myself in good shape, the more of that old, useless stuff I can leave behind.

> THE LAST STEP IN EMPTYING MENTAL TRASH IS TAKING CARE OF MY TRUCK.

Now, I'm not going to get into a ton of micro-details about how many fruits and vegetables you should eat or how many minutes of exercise you should do every day. Your doctor and your trainer know your body the best. They can help you create a maintenance plan that's made specifically for you and what you need. I'm here to tell you the basics: vegetables are better than donuts, and lifting the remote is not the same as lifting weights. When you treat yourself well, you'll keep pushing garbage out of your life. So get out your tools, roll up your sleeves, and get ready for a great lesson in basic maintenance and repair. Because nothing's better than a truck in perfect running condition.

THE FOUR BASICS

I've been in the waste industry for a long time and I've noticed that every company treats its trucks in a different way. Some rarely see the inside of a repair shop. Mechanical problems are ignored. Big maintenance items are deferred. Because the truck is in such poor shape, it's driven really hard, which makes some of its problems even worse. In some cases, it's a miracle that the truck is even on the road, let alone making it through a route.

The other type of garbage truck I've seen never misses any of its scheduled maintenance. Repairs are made at the first sign of trouble. All of the truck's systems are calibrated and work well together. Because the truck is in such good shape, it's driven carefully by anyone behind the wheel, which means it can easily handle anything the route throws at it.

I bounce back and forth between these two types of trucks. Sometimes I take really good care of my mind and my body, and sometimes I treat myself terribly. It depends on where my head is and what I'm up against at any given time. The challenge is keeping myself in good operating condition all the time, especially when I'm feeling like a wreck. To help me do that, I've boiled down truck care to four basic concepts. I've found that these keep me focused on the kind of truck I'd rather be driving: the one that rarely breaks down and always seems to get the job done. When my truck runs like that, I can get rid of my mental trash all day long.

1. Trucks don't last forever.

A truck is built to be on the road for a certain period of time. That's called its useful life. Plain and simple, the more I take care of myself, the more useful life I can get out of my body. I'm not saying that I can guarantee I'll live to be a hundred years old if I eat broccoli every day. What I mean is that I'll get more out of every day if I treat my body with care and respect.

> THE MORE I TAKE CARE OF MYSELF, THE MORE USEFUL LIFE I CAN GET OUT OF MY BODY.

That means there are certain things I do to keep myself in great shape. I stick to a reasonable diet. I get regular checkups. I stretch my mind with new ideas. I take quiet time to explore my spiritual side. These are all things that keep my head and my body in balance. It may not add decades to my life, but it sure improves the quality of the time that I have.

2. It's all important.

I used to wonder what the most important part of my garbage truck was: the engine, the brakes, or the oil. You know what I found out? *Every one* of those things is important. The whole truck is interconnected. If one part breaks, the entire truck is affected.

My body is no different. Exercising three times a week doesn't do me much good if half my meals come from fast food joints. Neither does creating new Empty Zones for myself by tossing outdated mental trash—but continuing to hoard a pile of nasty TBOs. Instead of arguing with myself about which system is more important, it makes more sense to develop a strategy to take care of all of them. For example, that may mean strengthening my back muscles because I drive so much, going to bed at a decent hour because I have to get up so early, and eating a lean diet to keep my weight down.

3. Know how the truck works.

If I'm going to be responsible for my own care and maintenance, I need to understand the specifics of how each system works. I wouldn't put gasoline in a diesel engine, just like I wouldn't eat French fries at every meal if I want to lose ten pounds.

That means I need to understand how all of my systems work together. How do changes in my diet affect my energy level? How much sleep do I need to avoid hitting that three o'clock wall of exhaustion? Taking care of my truck means understanding the little things that make me run well or that make me slow down and sputter. Reading the manual helps—in this case, hitting the Internet or reading books on health topics. (You should check out the Garbageman's Guide Owner's Manual at GG-Manual.com. Everyone reading this book is helping to create an online user's manual so we all get tips on better performance. Hop in and add your ideas, too!)

4. Don't underestimate the stress on the system.

If my boss told me to go out to a neighborhood and pick up a can here and a can there, my truck would have a pretty easy time of it. But if he tells me to empty 1,000–1,500 residential cans (a real number for many routes), that's going to put a lot of stress on the truck—and on me to get all that garbage collected in an eight-hour day.

Understanding my own stress points is critical if I don't want to damage myself. My top three are lack of preparation, making assumptions, and not following through. Any one of these sends my stress levels off the chart and creates a lot of unnecessary wear and tear—and I don't want the maintenance issues that come with that.

I once knew a woman named Sharon who was a full-on, type-A personality—a barn burner at work who always took on new projects and never minded putting in extra hours. I was always amazed at what she could accomplish in a week's time.

What I really admired though, was the way she kept everything in balance. Sure, she worked incredibly hard, but she also had a rock-solid commitment to taking care of herself. She taught a Zumba dance class at the gym near her house. She ate a lean diet. She spent time meditating and she followed a religious practice that helped keep her head clear and open. She told me that when life got crazy, the combination of physical exercise and quiet time helped her maintain

> *How much stress would you say is in your life? How much does it affect how you feel and how you act?*

her sanity. Whatever life threw at her, Sharon felt like she was ready to handle it. That was good, because life was about to change for her—in a big way.

ABUSE AND MISUSE

With an asset as important as my garbage truck, one of the primary goals is to get the most mileage out of it—not to push it like some old plow horse, but to treat it in such a way that it would give me the highest level of performance and longevity.

Having been a garbageman for so long, I've seen that longevity destroyed the moment drivers begin abusing the truck. If it's overloaded with too much garbage or if it's shaken like crazy by slamming heavy dumpsters around with the front forks, things start breaking really fast. I'm no different: When I overdo it by eating too much or blowing off my exercise routine, I can fall apart if I'm not careful.

Abuse is a nasty cycle. When I'm feeling depressed, I need to take *extra* good care of myself, both mentally and physically. But that's not what I do. I wolf down candy or knock back too many beers or stay up way too late watching junk on television. That may feel better in the short term, but it always ends up hurting me if I do it for too long.

Misuse is another way I hurt myself. Just like a garbage truck isn't built to be a race car, I'm not built to run a marathon. Sure, I could try, but I can tell you what'll happen: shin splints, sore knees, and some serious aches and pains. When I misuse my abilities and push myself into places I'm not meant to go, something usually breaks. I have to accept my limitations and stop abusing myself to the point of negligence. That's not helping anyone—least of all, me.

IGNORING THE WIRING

Let's say that the electrical system on my truck is working great and the engine is tuned and humming. However, I'm leaking hydraulic fluid, and the packer blade that compacts all the garbage isn't working well. That flaw is going to affect the operation of the whole truck, even though the other systems are working fine.

> REMEMBER THE MIND-BODY CONNECTION? THAT REALLY COMES INTO PLAY HERE.

Remember the mind-body connection? That really comes into play here. If I've learned anything about dealing with mental trash, it's that my mind and my body are tightly wired together. I know that sounds weird—one is physical and the other is intangible—but what I think and what I feel usually shows up in my body. If I'm really worried about something, I almost always get a headache. If I'm stacking up mental garbage, my stomach twists itself in knots and I'm chowing down antacids like there's no tomorrow. Think about it. My brain creates all my thoughts and emotions and that brain is part of my body. How can they not be wired together?

Pretend that I give all my focus to taking care of my physical self. I run every day, I eat well, and I get all the rest I need. If I don't toss my mental trash or take some time to reflect or explore the spiritual side of life, my mind never gets a break. If it's frazzled, there's no way I can stay on my route, no matter how well my body is functioning. It's like training for a 10K race while being hounded by totally destructive TBOs like *I'm a crummy athlete* and *I'm too old to run like this*. Sure, my body will get in shape, but my mind is going to fight me every step of the way. Who wants that?

The opposite is also true. If I put all my energy into my mind, my body is going to take a beating. Let's say I can join a gym and my mind tells me that I can start lifting heavy weights right away. Guess what? I'm going to hurt myself. If my mind says that I don't need any mental downtime and I can work insane hours every day, how long do you think my body will last if it's deprived of sleep and fed a steady diet of coffee and energy drinks? I can't tell you how many times I've come home and said to my wife, "I feel like I've been dragged through the mud." Ten to one, it's not because I just finished running ten miles. It's because my mind is overworked and stressed and hasn't had a minute of downtime to regroup and recharge. And where does all that show up? That's right: in my body.

Here's the bottom line: I can't ignore the wiring. These two systems—mind and body—are linked together just like brakes and tires. The more I respect that and keep the two in balance, the better I'll end up feeling in the long run.

Remember Sharon? Almost without warning, things started to change at her company. It began raining orders from customers and sales went through the roof. Work hours began to stretch. Stress levels began climbing. Everyone was running around like crazy, trying to respond to this explosion of growth. Sharon was promoted and sent on the road to help the regional sales offices deal with all the new changes.

Sharon knew that extensive travel was going to mean a mega-interruption to her normal routine. She knew that airports, longs hours, and a heavy workload could take over her life if she wasn't careful. So she mapped out a plan: how she was going to eat, how often she was going to exercise, and how she was going to find time for relaxation and for her spiritual practices. She packed her bag, headed to the airport, and caught the first flight to her new life.

NO TWO ARE THE SAME

On the surface, it seems like every garbage truck is exactly the same. They're all built from a master blueprint, they contain the same parts, and they're all put together in the same way. Look a little closer though, and you'll see that there are slight variations in how the nuts are tightened, the quality of the wire on any given day, and imperfections in the steel. All of these tiny differences affect how each truck will perform over its lifetime.

The same thing is true of people. We all pretty much have the same parts—a heart, a liver, bones, and blood—and we're all made the same way—conception, growth, and birth. But that's where the similarity ends. Genetics, family history, race, and gender are just some of the factors that will cause differences in performance as we make our way through our life.

While I can't change things like my genetics, I do have control over how I take care of myself. If I pound the accelerator, jam on the brakes, and screech around life's corners until nuts and bolts are flying out of me, I can guarantee that any imperfection in my body is going to be magnified. I'm not suggesting that I come home from work, sit down on the couch, and fold my hands so I don't risk overdoing it. It's all about moderation and common sense. If I know I have certain issues with my body, it's reasonable not to do things that could make it worse.

DEALING WITH BREAKDOWNS

Tell me if this sounds familiar. I do everything that I'm supposed to: drive my garbage truck carefully, take it to the shop for regular service, and check my systems every day during my pre- and post-trip inspections. Then, right in the middle of my route, *bam!* Something breaks and my entire day is screwed up. And of course, this always happens at the absolute worst time, as if the breakdown gods are all conspiring against me.

> BREAKDOWNS ALWAYS HAPPEN AT THE ABSOLUTE WORST TIME.

The same thing happens to me outside of work. Sometimes it's getting the flu or spraining an ankle or dealing with a kid who suddenly decides to act up in school. These breakdowns seem to come out of nowhere, and their timing is usually terrible. I mean, why is it that three or four really big bills always hit me right when I have the least amount of cash to pay them?

Despite the fact that this has happened to me my whole adult life, I'm still caught off guard by breakdowns. I get angry when they happen, as if somehow I should be above such mundane things. Well, I'm not immortal, and I'm not the president or a famous rock star. I'm a regular old guy with problems just like everyone else. Life is going to throw me a few flat tires and it's much better to deal with them head on instead of running around yelling that the sky is falling.

Let's get back to Sharon. Three months into her new job, she was a wreck. She was lucky to find five hours of sleep a night. Eating became feast or famine: overeating lousy hotel food or skipping meals altogether. She'd grab exercise when she could, but even that became a challenge. All this new responsibility was eating her alive.

She wasn't helping herself, either. She'd go out late with the office staff, have too much to drink, and come to the office the next morning bleary-eyed and foggy. In her usual take-no-prisoners style, Sharon pushed herself like there was no tomorrow. She knew that she was overdoing it, but she couldn't stop. There was so much work to do and it was her responsibility to manage it all. She was a breakdown waiting to happen…and she knew it.

Here's the bottom line. If I party every night, drink too much, and smoke cigarettes, I know what effect that will have on the way I feel, the same way I can predict what will happen if I watch my cholesterol and dump my mental trash. That's not a good or a bad thing. It's purely cause and effect. So that means self-maintenance isn't rocket science or open-heart surgery. It's common sense. If I take good care of myself, I can spend more time on the road moving along the route to the life I really want.

> SELF-MAINTENANCE ISN'T ROCKET SCIENCE OR OPEN-HEART SURGERY. IT'S COMMON SENSE.

THE ART OF ADAPTING

Garbage trucks are made up of two main parts: the frame and the body. The body is the garbage collector and sits on top of the frame, which contains the cab, the engine, the transmission, and the wheels.

A few years back, our company bought a bunch of new trucks with the latest and greatest bodies on them. However, they were so heavy that the truck felt like it was half-loaded with trash even though it was completely empty. Here's what we found. If we weren't careful, under certain circumstances, the rear axle on the frame could snap if you let the clutch out wrong.

Now, you'd think we would have had a bunch of broken axles, wouldn't you? Well, that's not what happened. The drivers knew there was a vulnerability and they adapted their clutch skills. So instead of a bunch of expensive repairs, we got improved drivers who handled those trucks like they were pieces of expensive art.

> IF I HAVE A WEAKNESS, TAKING CARE OF MYSELF MEANS I LEARN HOW TO ADAPT TO IT.

If I know I have a weakness, taking care of myself means learning how to adapt to it. For example, I'm lactose intolerant, so I've learned to stay away from certain foods that upset my stomach. My son used to pull his hamstring when he ran track, so he learned to stretch a certain way to stop it from seizing up. Weaknesses don't have to be showstoppers. It's a matter of knowing they're there and putting a plan in place to work around them.

When I was young, I went ten years with nothing more than a bad cold, so I suckered myself into believing that I was different from everyone else. They're the ones who needed exercise and diets—not me. Then, my waistline started expanding, my cholesterol went through the roof, and running a couple of miles became a lot harder than it used to be. That's when I began to realize that I couldn't keep driving myself a hundred miles an hour. I had to be accountable to this body that was going to be with me for the rest of my life. If I expected a high level of performance from it, then I had to treat it with care and respect.

When it's all said and done, I'm headed for the scrap heap. I don't know when it will happen, but believe me, it will. Knowing that, there's a lot I can do to take care of myself along the way. By accepting the fact that I'm responsible for my own care and maintenance, I can make some good choices about how I treat my mind and my body. My mom lived by the same philosophy and she made it to ninety-two, so I believe there's something to this idea.

That's why I pay attention to all my weaknesses and do my best to adapt to them.

It was almost five months to the day since Sharon had first hit the road. One morning, her back hurt, so she sat on the carpeted floor in her hotel room and stretched, finalizing a PowerPoint presentation for a meeting at the same time. She showered, grabbed her stuff, and headed out for another long day at the office.

As the hours dragged on, she noticed a nagging pain in her hips. Sitting was getting increasingly uncomfortable and she wondered what was going on. Back at her hotel room fourteen hours later, she got undressed and looked at herself in the bathroom mirror. A nasty, purple bruise had formed that ran from her butt all the way to the small of her back. She had lost so much weight and body fat that sitting on the carpet had bruised her tailbone.

As she stared at the injury, she took stock of where she was. Her brain was fried. She couldn't remember the last time she had been to religious services or listened to the meditation app on her phone. Exercising had gone out the window, as had any semblance of decent eating habits. She looked at her backside and realized how symbolic the injury was. Because she had stopped taking care of herself, she hadn't just bruised her body. She had also bruised her mind, her sense of balance, and her sanity. And she had finally had enough.

WEAR SPOTS

Every truck has wear spots, places where seals break and metal grinds against metal, or where a wire gets pinched inside the harness and a light keeps flickering on and off. If I don't have the shop take care of these wear spots, they eventually become chronic problems that can create havoc for me.

Some wear spots are buried deep inside my truck, which makes them difficult to diagnose. Once I discover where they are, finding a fix can be equally as challenging. While it takes effort and can be a pain sometimes, here's what I know: ignoring wear spots is not an option if I expect my garbage truck to run well.

What are some of my most common wear spots?

- Tough conversations that I won't have

- Important medical procedures that I keep putting off, like a prostate exam or a colonoscopy

- Bad relationships at work that sit there and fester

- A pain in my body I won't get looked at or a chronic problem in my mind that I won't get help with

These wear spots grind away at my performance. They steal a bit of effectiveness here or decision-making capability there. Like a slow oil leak, this adds up over time until it becomes a real problem that could threaten my overall health.

Getting rid of wear spots feels great. It's one of those things in life that I don't realize how much it was actually bothering me until it's gone. When I finally stop procrastinating and cross some of those chronic to-dos off my list, I feel such

Where are your wear spots? How would life be different if you got rid of them?

a huge sense of relief. No more friction. No more energy nagging at myself. No more fears about the consequences of not acting. That part of my mind is now free to do other far more important things—like dumping mental trash and creating some much-needed Empty Zones for myself.

A MORE EFFECTIVE TEAM

It might seem like taking care of my mind and my body is all about me, but it's not.

When I'm running at full capacity, people around me don't have to pick up my slack, at work or at home. No one has to create contingency plans or scramble to fill in the gap because I'm breaking down all the time. I'm the guy they can count on to keep myself in good running condition. That means they're free to work on their own maintenance instead of worrying about how to carry part of my load.

Let me tell you, I hate being a burden to other people. Everyone's busy enough without weighing them down with my preventable maintenance issues. I'm not saying that I don't lean on my team when I need them. They're there for me, and I'm there for them. By keeping myself in good shape though, I can balance the times I need them with the times I can give back to them, so it's not a one-way street—in either direction.

MAINTENANCE BENEFIT LIST

I wanted to have a little fun with this idea of taking care of my truck, so I read through a bunch of repair manuals the shop mechanic loaned me and made a list of every benefit I could find that dealt with maintenance. I took that list and applied it to the idea of keeping myself in really good shape. Here's what I came up with.

- **More uptime.** I'm on the road getting things done instead of in the shop recuperating.

- **Increased productivity.** The better I run, the more I can accomplish.

- **Reduced overtime.** Burning the midnight oil becomes the exception, not the rule.

- **Improved efficiency.** When I'm well tuned, I can produce more with less fuel, energy, and waste.

- **Strengthened reputation.** I'm the guy people can count on rather than the guy who always breaks down.

- **Optimized limited resources.** There's only one of me. The better care I give myself, the more I can find and get rid of wasteful activities and focus on the stuff that really matters.

- **Established standard for acceptable performance.** Once I commit to maintaining myself, I create a benchmark that says, "I won't go below this level"—and I can measure myself to that benchmark.

- **Improved quality.** Because I'm more focused, I make fewer mistakes and I get more dependable, higher-quality results.

- **Easier error detection.** The more I check myself for issues, the more familiar I get with how I work—which means I can spot errors and problems faster and easier.

- **Improved safety.** When I'm not exhausted and falling apart, I'm much less likely to cause an accident.

- **Lowered expenses.** When I'm taking good care of myself, I have fewer medical bills and lost wages.

- **Decreased pressure to perform.** When I'm tuned up well, there's no pressure to perform because I know my capabilities and my limits.

- **Better support and service.** If I'm not wrapped up in my own maintenance issues, I'm more available to help other people.

- **Extended equipment life.** The better I take care of myself, the longer useful life I can expect.

- **Increased accountability.** Taking care of myself means people can count on me to deliver what I promise.

How's that for an inspirational list? With so many benefits, it's clear that taking care of myself is central to emptying my mental trash. When my body and mind are tuned up and working in sync, any negative TBO that's trying to tear me down is going to stand out like it's ringed in neon. I don't need it, I don't want it, and it belongs in the trash, not in my head. That's how I keep myself out of the dumps.

MAINTENANCE AND REPAIR CHECKLIST

My dad used to tell me that it's much better to put a fence at the top of the cliff than an ambulance at the bottom. When it comes to taking care of my truck, that's about the best advice I can get. I'd rather deal with my issues—mental and physical—sooner rather than later, before they can mushroom into catastrophic problems. I need to keep throwing out my mental trash, and I can't do that if my truck is broken down on the side of the road. So, I've put together my own Maintenance and Repair Checklist that's designed to take care of my truck and keep me in good shape.

1. **Cover the basics.**
    - ✓ Eat a healthy diet.
    - ✓ Exercise on a regular basis, every week.
    - ✓ Don't go to bed mad.
    - ✓ Use restraint and moderation when I'm doing things I know are bad for me.
    - ✓ Take a break when I'm feeling worn out.
    - ✓ Never take my body and my mind for granted. They can break if they're abused, mistreated, or ignored.

2. **If it's broken, fix it.**
   - ✓ Fix anything that's not working well—which means ending the practice of putting off repairs. If something won't stop hurting, I'll go to the doctor. If I haven't phoned a good friend for a few weeks, I'll make the call. Taking care of repairs stops the problem from worsening and stops the endless nagging in my head: *I really need to do something about that!*
   - ✓ Every truck has chronic issues: a rattle that won't go away or a persistent oil leak. I have them, too: a feeling of dread before every staff meeting or a problem with a friend or a family member. Unless I love anxiety, I need to stop ignoring the chronic issues and get them fixed.

3. **Schedule preventative maintenance.**
   - ✓ Make a preventative maintenance checklist: what needs to get done (e.g., mammograms, prostate exams) and how often they should be performed (daily, weekly, monthly, annually).
   - ✓ Schedule the appointment. Even if it's a year out, get it on the calendar. It's one less wear spot to worry about.
   - ✓ Make the necessary preparations. Some preventative maintenance procedures need special preparation, like laying off food, alcohol, or activities. It's a pain to give it up, but it's a lot better than getting sick.

4. **Find and fix the wear spots.**
   - ✓ Constantly check for points of friction at work, at home, with relationships, and with my personal truck.
   - ✓ Determine the best kind of "oil" to use: a conversation, a letter, a mediated discussion, a change in exercise or diet.

✓ Apply the oil, remembering that it might take more than one treatment in the beginning before I see progress.

✓ Follow up regularly. Has the friction eased up or does it need more attention?

5. **Always be safe.**

✓ Check myself for safety issues that could lead to accidents: excess anger or frustration, relationships that need fixing, or important issues that I'm ignoring.

✓ Watch out for momentum, so I don't creep into unwanted areas or lose control of my truck and find myself in places I don't want to be.

✓ Never exceed my factory tolerances unless I'm properly prepared, trained, and protected. In other words, don't sign up for a triathlon with only two weeks of training.

6. **Schedule preventative maintenance during downtime.**

✓ Preventative maintenance requires my undivided attention. Taking a five-minute mental timeout during the day is great. However, attempting major preventative maintenance—mental or physical—in the car rushing to an appointment will get me less than stellar results.

✓ Schedule downtime on my calendar just like any other appointment. Make a date night. Take time out for church or synagogue. Block off a half-hour meditation. Failure to set aside specific time for my preventative maintenance means that it won't get done!

✓ Avoid distractions during my maintenance cycle. Turn off all cell phones, computers, televisions, and other devices. No interruptions are allowed except in the case of emergencies!

USE CAUTION

To make sure I'm taking care of my truck, I need to keep an eye out for two things: being a team player and remembering that tune-ups take time.

BE A TEAM PLAYER

My preventative maintenance routine includes checking in with other people. I make it a point to find out what issues they're having and I offer to pick up a wrench and help out with any repairs they may need. This give-and-take builds really strong relationships and makes me as valuable to them as they are to me.

Checking in with my team also helps me avoid the "showroom effect": getting fooled because their lives look so immaculate and polished. Listen, I never know what's going on under someone else's hood. They may be struggling with a significant issue, and I would never know it if I don't make the effort to look beyond the gleaming façade. That's what checking in does: it gives me a chance to help, even if the other person is trying to hide issues from me.

> I NEVER KNOW WHAT'S GOING ON UNDER SOMEONE ELSE'S HOOD.

The last thing I have to remember is not to take my desire to be a team player to an extreme. I'm not a fleet manager. It's not my responsibility to fix everyone and everything around me. My job is to balance my maintenance needs with that of my team. That's the best way to make sure everyone stays on the road.

TUNE-UPS TAKE TIME

You've heard me say this before: I've been collecting mental trash for decades, so it's unrealistic to think that I can dump it all at once. The same thing is true with taking care of myself. If I've been misusing or abusing my health, or I blow off my Maintenance and Repair Checklist, it's going to take some time before I get myself back on track again.

That doesn't mean it can't be done. Smokers who quit see improvements to their lungs and their blood pressure. People who cut fast food and high-calorie sweets out of their diet lose excess weight. Damage can be reversed. However, it's not going to happen in a day or a week. It's going to take time, which is unfortunate because I want results right now!

The best example of this I can give is Sharon. It was clear that she had completely lost the balance between her job and taking care of herself. To fix this, she put a new plan in place. She started delegating more work to her staff and used the freed-up hours to hit the gym and take some mental quiet time for herself. She found a way to eat better on the road and she stopped saying yes to every single request that came her way. It took a few months, but her body and her mind began to recover. She told me that the strangest part of it all was that she was able to accomplish more with less wear and tear. Things still got crazy, but this time she didn't sacrifice her commitment to take care of herself. And that, she said, made all the difference.

TAKING IT TO THE STREET

SUMMARY: TAKE CARE OF YOUR TRUCK

If my garbage truck sounds like a wheezing elephant and the hydraulics can barely lift a garbage can, emptying people's trash is going to be very difficult. Sure, I can get through my route, but imagine how much easier it would be if I weren't afraid the wheels were going to fall off. If I want efficiency, performance, and safety out of my truck, I have to make sure the proper care is put into it.

My body works the exact same way. It's totally unrealistic of me to expect Olympic-sized results from my life if I treat myself like an old mule. Abuse and misuse are two of the biggest culprits behind lousy performance. Not accepting the link between my mind and my body means one or both will suffer if they don't receive decent care. And the expectation that I should never experience a breakdown is laughable given how badly I can treat myself sometimes.

THE BACKBONE OF TAKING CARE OF MY TRUCK IS THE UNDERSTANDING OF CAUSE AND EFFECT.

The backbone of taking care of my truck is the understanding of cause and effect. The better I maintain myself, the better I'll run. That makes life a lot easier for my team and for me. They spend less time worrying about my problems and I can spend more time helping them with theirs.

The list of benefits from good personal maintenance is long and very attractive. From more efficiency to improved safety, taking care of my truck means my mind is free to focus on a far more important task: getting rid of my mental trash.

EXERCISES

1. **Focus on just one aspect of your life that really needs care and maintenance. It can be something specific—a pain that won't go away in your ankle—or something broader like improving your diet. Write it down.**

_____

_____

_____

_____

_____

_____

_____

2. Make a list of the specific steps that are needed to fix the problem: people you need to see, books you need to read, or other actions that will help you get the problem under control.

_____

_____

_____

_____

_____

3. Once the problem is fixed, write down the preventative maintenance steps you need to take to minimize the chances of the problem returning.

_____

_____

_____

_____

_____

4. Schedule each step of your preventative maintenance. Put the appointments on your calendar, whether they're with someone else (doctor visit or gym tour) or with yourself (fifteen-minute meditation). Make sure to schedule downtime, when you can really focus on getting the results you want.

_____

_____

CONCLUSION

"Difficulties mastered are opportunities won."
—Winston Churchill

When I was a little kid facing a big, huge world on my own, almost everything that happened to me was new and strange. My young, inexperienced mind had a tough time making sense of it all—especially the emotions that I felt. To help me keep my sanity, I created thoughts, beliefs, and opinions about what was happening around me. Were most of these TBOs accurate? Was the belief *I must be stupid* the real reason why I got creamed in my first spelling bee? Not really, but it didn't matter. Creating TBOs helped me cope.

Gradually, as the years ticked by, I realized that I didn't lose the spelling bee because I was stupid. Most people in sixth grade have a tough time spelling "baccalaureate." Once my mind realized this, it intellectually let go of the *I must be stupid* TBO. However, the emotional side of it never quite left me. That's because feelings can be much stronger than logic. As a result, every time I have some kind of failure—I can't fix a leaky faucet or I don't get a raise—the

I must be stupid TBO pops up and I feel like that sixth grade kid all over again.

It sounds silly, doesn't it? The TBO is old. It's negative. It was formed when I was a child and it has absolutely no relevance to my adult life. It's mental garbage. Yet, no one ever taught me that if I want that TBO to stop bothering me, I have to intentionally throw it out the same way I do my physical garbage. That was a revelation to me—and I get rid of trash for a living! Once I realized that the same skills I use to get rid of garbage in the real world can be used to get rid of the garbage in my head, things began to change. That's why this book was written: to show you that a whole new life is possible just by dumping your mental trash.

You see, as a garbageman, I see the pain people go through—the changes in their lives, the movement from one stage to another—all from the garbage that they get rid of. It really is true: the flow of trash and the flow of life are nearly identical. That's where *The Garbageman's Guide to Life* philosophy comes from: the eight simple steps we all can use to get rid of the trash in our minds.

To translate that philosophy to hardcore, life-changing results, I've learned to monitor the thousands of thoughts that cross my mind every day. It's so easy to fall asleep to them, to stop noticing the negative messages they keep bringing and to blindly accept them as the absolute truth. Time and time again, I've seen that *what I think is who I believe I am*. Well, if half my thoughts are old, destructive TBOs, no wonder I'm in the dumps so often!

What if I could change what's in my mind and replace all those old TBOs with brand new ones that have a totally different message? That's called taking out my mental garbage. Once I'm free from all that old thinking, my behavior changes. I feel a sense of purpose and the goals I set out for myself don't seem nearly as tough to reach. The more I think of old TBOs as garbage, the easier it is for me to get them out of my head and out of my life.

Listen, I instinctively know what's garbage and what isn't. Why not leverage that knowledge and apply it to all the junk I'm carrying in my mind? Taking out the mental trash allows me to stop the chaos and move toward something that's open and clutter-free. I can see when a TBO is interfering in my career, my relationships, or my family. It's pretty amazing: I can learn from my past without having my feet anchored in it. To me, that's the formula for an extraordinary life.

Thinking of TBOs as trash helps me separate out what's valuable from what contaminates me. It lets me create an open, exciting future that's not polluted with every single thing I ever did wrong. Throwing out my mental garbage sometimes means letting go of strongly held opinions I have about myself. However, if those opinions are truly inaccurate and outdated, why would I keep them anymore? They don't represent the person I know I want to be and I don't want to be chained up by them anymore.

> THINKING OF TBOS AS TRASH HELPS ME SEPARATE OUT WHAT'S VALUABLE FROM WHAT CONTAMINATES ME.

True change comes when I believe with all my heart that I can become a different person. Once I set my sights on that new vision of myself, I see my thoughts in a whole new light: They're either garbage or they're not, and I use value to help me figure that out. If a TBO doesn't line up with the person I want to become, it gets thrown out, right then and there. Think about it! If the only thing standing in the way of my dreams and me is a bunch of mental garbage, I'm in great shape because *I already know how to get rid of trash.* All I have to do is put those same skills to work on the contents of my head and before I know it, I am that person I dreamed about—and I have the life I've always wanted.

At the end of the day, I have to get myself out of the dumps. No one can do it for me. As long as I believe that someone or something else is responsible for creating my mental garbage, I'll never throw it away and move beyond it. Will old trash come back and stick to me again? Absolutely. Will I hoard some of it when I hit a speed bump? It happens all the time. But that doesn't stop me anymore because this is *my* route, *my* choice, *my* path. My garbage is no longer in control of my life. *I* am.

This is the way of the garbageman. It's taking the keep-or-toss decisions I've been making for decades and applying them to the contents of my mind. To help me remember how to do this, here's a quick recap of the eight steps and their action plans.

STEP 1: FIND THE VALUE AND TOSS THAT TRASH

THE VALUE SERVICE PLAN

1. Create a Value Filter.

2. Run TBOs through my Value Filter.

3. Toss that trash.

4. Keep making trips to the landfill.

STEP 2: KEEP IT EMPTY

THE EMPTY AND RETURN ACTION PLAN

1. Go clean something—outside.

2. Go clean something—inside.

3. Find eight minutes of emptiness.

4. Get used to the discomfort of emptiness.

5. Guard the Empty Zone.

STEP 3: CREATE YOUR ROUTE

ROUTE MANAGEMENT SYSTEM

1. Figure out where I am.

2. Figure out where I want to be.

3. Engage my belief system.

4. Physically exit the comfort zone.

5. Mentally exit the comfort zone.

STEP 4: PARK YOUR EGO

THE PARKSAFE ACTION PLAN

1. Do an audit.

2. Stop talking and start listening.

3. Build a team.

4. Practice humility.

STEP 5: LEAVE IT IN THE LANDFILL

THE LANDFILL MANAGEMENT PROGRAM

1. Identify the mental contracts that I've linked to persistent TBOs.

2. Run the persistent TBO through an enhanced Value Filter.

3. Initiate a Forgiveness Cycle.

4. If it's appropriate, take action.

5. Remember that forgiveness, like emptying garbage, is a process and not an event.

STEP 6: GET AWAY FROM TOXIC WASTE

Toxic Waste Action Plan

1. Practice the drill.

2. Low-level toxic waste: Read the label.

3. High-level toxic waste: Suit up and get away.

STEP 7: STOP HOARDING

Hoarding School

1. Figure out what I'm hoarding—and why.

2. Isolate the junk.

3. Let it go.

4. Get help.

STEP 8: TAKE CARE OF YOUR TRUCK

Maintenance and Repair Checklist

1. Cover the basics.

2. If it's broken, fix it.

3. Schedule preventative maintenance.

4. Find and fix the wear spots.

5. Always be safe.

6. Schedule preventative maintenance during downtime.

As we reach the end of our journey together, I invite you to visit the website GG-Resources.com. You'll find a ton of ways you can take these eight steps even further. The more you learn, the more of your own garbage you'll be able to dump.

There's an old saying that people don't change because they see the light, but rather because they feel the heat. So much of that heat comes from the garbage that we allow to pile up in our minds. All we need to do is the noble work of the garbageman: Toss anything that has no more value. That's what I wish for you—a happy, joyous life in which old garbage never bothers you again.

GLOSSARY

"Always remember that striving and struggle precede success, even in the dictionary."
—Sarah Ban Breathnach

I've thrown a lot of new terms at you, so I thought I'd pull them all together in one place so you can quickly review them. One note: These aren't dictionary definitions of these words, but rather the specific way we use them in this book.

AFFIRMATION
An action or statement that paints a picture in my mind of a new place I want to be in my life.

BELIEF SYSTEM
The part of my mind that believes with 100 percent certainty that I have already become the person of my goals and dreams, even though I may not actually be there yet.

BLIND SPOT
An area in my life where I'm blind to the effects of my own behavior.

CHAOS

The disorder and confusion that I feel when I don't have a defined route for myself and when my ego is in charge.

COMFORT ZONE

The part of my mind that avoids risk and sets mental boundaries in order to feel secure and in control of the world around me.

DRAMA

The unnecessary conflict and stress I create when my ego is in control or I'm hoarding certain destructive TBOs.

EGO

The me-centric portion of my personality that resists change, does not like expanding my comfort zone, and relies on my past to make sense of what's happening in the here and now. The ego is the opposite of my Inner Garbageman.

EMPTINESS

The space in my mind that opens up when I throw away a thought, belief, or opinion about a certain topic. I use emptiness to create a new way to look at that topic, now that the old way of thinking is gone.

EMPTY ZONE

An area of emptiness.

FAÇADE

The false front created by the ego, where the personality trait that I'm showing the world is covering up what's I'm actually thinking and feeling.

FORGIVENESS

The act of letting go of my connection to the event(s) that created a certain thought, belief, or opinion.

FORGIVENESS CYCLE

A process designed to break the emotional contract I have with an event from my past and the TBOs that I made up around it.

GARBAGE

A thought, belief, or opinion that no longer has any value to me.

GOAL

A target I'm choosing for myself in the future that changes how I act or think in one of my segments today.

HIGH-LEVEL TOXIC WASTE

A special category of mental garbage composed of personality traits, behaviors, or relationships that are very destructive, can easily contaminate others, and generally require professional intervention to contain and clean up.

HOARDING

The inability to assign value to a collection of TBOs in one of my segments. Because I can't figure out which of these TBOs are garbage, I hold on to all of them.

INNER GARBAGEMAN

The part of my personality that takes risk, steps out of my comfort zone, and does not maintain a relationship with my past, thereby allowing me to toss my mental trash. My Inner Garbageman is the opposite of my ego.

LANDFILL

The final resting spot in my mind for all of the thoughts, beliefs, and opinions that no longer have any value to me.

LOW-LEVEL TOXIC WASTE

A special type of mental garbage that carries a mild to moderate risk of contamination and whose side effects are generally confined to me.

MASK

A specific set of reactions used by my ego to hide what I'm actually feeling or thinking.

PREVENTATIVE MAINTENANCE

A set of behaviors and actions designed to keep me well and stop certain preventable health problems from occurring.

REACTION

An emotional thought or action that kicks in automatically when I run into a situation that I've seen or felt before.

RESPONSE

A non-emotional, reasoned thought or action.

ROUTE

A planned pathway from the place I am now to a goal that I have set for myself.

SEGMENT

A specific part of my life, such as Career, Family, or Hobby.

SIDE TRIP

A thought or action that distracts me from the route I set toward a certain goal, and sends me in a different, non-productive direction.

TBO

A thought, belief, or opinion I have about a certain aspect of my life that I made while reacting to a key personality-forming event.

TEAM

Friends, family, and professionals whom I lean on to help me achieve my goals and stay on my route.

TRASH TRIGGER

A feeling, situation, or event that causes a strong emotional re-action that makes me want to resurrect a TBO that I already threw into my landfill.

TRUCK

A metaphor for my body.

VALUE

The amount of worth and importance found in a TBO.

VALUE CRITERIA

A set of questions I ask in order to see how much value is in a specific TBO I'm carrying around in my mind.

VALUE FILTER

A tool I use to separate out the TBOs that are garbage from the TBOs that I want to keep.

WEAR SPOT

A thought, situation, or person that always causes me stress, anxiety, or other undesirable emotions or reactions.

ACKNOWLEDGMENTS

Norm LeMay

I first wish to acknowledge my mother, Alberta, who worked on a garbage route with her father while she was pregnant with me. That gave me the earliest possible start in the industry!

I want to acknowledge my father, Harold, whose foresight created a garbage company of which I was proud to be a part.

I also have received support and help from my brother, Eugene LeMay, and Lynn Grubbs, both of whom valiantly worked with me in the early phase of this wonderful project.

Finally, I'd like to thank my family, friends, and industry associates, all of whom have listened to my personal philosophy and have helped deepen and mature my understanding of *The Garbageman's Guide to Life*.

Steven Kaufman

I would like to thank my father, Julian Kaufman, and my sisters, Karen Kaufman and Linda McDonald, for their unyielding support, guidance, and encouragement to create my own route.

I'd also like to acknowledge the memory of my mother, Carole Kaufman, whose exuberance and gentle spirit helped me discover my Inner Garbageman.

I'd like to thank David Hancock and Terry Whalin of Morgan James Publishing for believing in our project and Amanda Rooker and Bonnie Mitchell for turning an edit of our manuscript into an art form.

To Sandi Serling and John Heitkemper, thank you for bringing our message to the world and for your unending well of enthusiasm, energy, and love.

Finally, this book would not have been possible without the countless hours of sage advice, consultation, and enthusiastic backing of my friends and colleagues. Your contribution to this work is immeasurable. To each of you, I am deeply indebted and profoundly grateful.

ABOUT THE AUTHORS

Co-authors Norm LeMay and Steven Kaufman are two guys who love talking trash.

Norm LeMay is an entrepreneur, educator, and philosopher. Thanks to his unique approach to management, he spent thirty years of his storied career helping to convert his family's business—a waste management company that his father picked up in a swap for an old truck—into an asset worth more than $300 million. Through hard work and foresight, LeMay became a pioneer in recycling, converting the state of Washington into one of the most efficient recycling areas in the United States.

Steven Kaufman, known among friends as a brainiac with an incessant curiosity, graduated with honors from Stanford University. He spent the first twenty years of his varied career with companies like Wang and Intel, tackling assignments in the US, Europe, and Asia. In 2000, he shifted lanes and became an entrepreneur and a consultant, helping to launch a high tech company that developed an automated route tracking system for the waste industry.

Working with garbage every day taught Norm and Steven that we all carry trash in our heads that gets in the way of our relationships, our jobs, and our dreams. By taking the basics of the trash business—the truck, the landfill, the can—Norm and Steven, known as the Disposal Dream Team™, have developed a down-to-earth philosophy to toss that trash and go on to live an extraordinary life.

You've Finished the Book. Now Put It to Work!

Congratulations! You've finished *The Garbageman's Guide to Life*. If the idea of dumping your mental trash and creating a whole new way of thinking is exciting to you, there's a world of resources that will take your knowledge to a new level!

Enter this web address in your Internet browser:

www.GG-Resources.com

Complete the short order form and you'll get access to:

- Videos that expand on key topics from the book
- Special reader emails
- Articles that dive deeper into tossing mental trash
- Exclusive audio content just for readers

There's also the Garbageman's Guide to Life Companion Guide, invitations to webinars, in-person courses, and so much more! Have a look at the website and keep tossing your mental trash—every day!

CPSIA information can be obtained at www.ICGtesting.com
Printed in the USA
BVOW07s0701130114

341378BV00002B/6/P